The Big Questions

The Big
Questions

HOW TO FIND YOUR
OWN ANSWERS TO LIFE'S
ESSENTIAL MYSTERIES

by Lama Surya Das

RODALE

Rodale books may be purchased for business or promotional use or for special
sales. For information, please write to:

Special Markets Department, Rodale, Inc., 733 Third Avenue,
New York, NY 10017

Printed in the United States of America

Rodale Inc. makes every effort to use acid-free ♾, recycled paper ♲.

Book design by Christina Gaugler

Library of Congress Cataloging-in-Publication Data

Surya Das, Lama
 The big questions : how to find your own answers to life's essential
mysteries / by Lama Surya Das.
  p.   cm.
 ISBN-13 978–1–59486–208–3 hardcover
 ISBN-10 1–59486–208–7 hardcover
 1. Spiritual life—Buddhism. I. Title.
 BQ5660.S87 2007
 294.3'4—dc22   2007031098

Distributed to the book trade by Holtzbrinck Publishers

2 4 6 8 10 9 7 5 3 1   hardcover

*The important thing is
not to stop questioning.*

—ALBERT EINSTEIN

TABLE OF CONTENTS

A questioning man is halfway to being wise.

—IRISH SAYING

Life is an unanswered question, but let's still believe in the
dignity and importance of the question.

—TENNESSEE WILLIAMS

The Sacred Art of Questioning

Every life is a journey through the unknown. Along the way, we can't avoid confronting the same perplexing mysteries again and again. Some are cosmic enigmas, the Big Questions that have always teased the human mind: What is my purpose in life? What happens after I die? Why are we here, where do we come from, and where are we going? How shall I live my life? What is my relationship to the ever-present idea of God and other seemingly impenetrable mysteries of life and death, truth and reality, time, space, and eternity? Others are puzzles laid at our feet by present-day society: How far should sexual freedom extend? What is my personal responsibility to the poor, the hungry and the homeless, and to the global environment?

Popular culture tries to get us interested in cracking enigmas like the Da Vinci code or, more importantly, the genetic codes that might lead to finding cures for disease. What about breaking through our personal identity codes and developing character, integrity, ethics, and personal values? What about untangling teenager codes, in-law codes, workplace codes, gender codes, dress codes, and other enigmas of everyday life? Then there are the science-focused questions, including the origins of the material universe; the nature of time, space, and infinity; and the mysterious birth of life.

It was Socrates, the father of Western philosophy, who lectured the public: "Citizens of Athens: Aren't you ashamed to be concerned so much about making all the money you can and advancing your reputation and prestige, while for truth and wisdom and the improvement of your souls you have no thought or care?" He was soon convicted of corrupting the youth of that city, and sentenced to death.

Plato believed that the sources of philosophy are wonder and discovery. He posed several of the seminal Great Questions, which he learned to value from his master, Socrates, who famously exhorted his disciples to "Know thyself."

Plato wanted to know:

- What is the nature of reality?

- What is truth? Beauty? Virtue?

- What is the best political system?

- What are the limits of knowledge?

- What is courage? Justice? Moderation?

Bill Moyers, my favorite journalist, said, "Every journalist worth his or her salt knows that the towering question of our time is 'What is the human spirit?'" Jean Jacques Rousseau asked, "Why is everyone unhappy?" French philosopher Blaise Pascal said: "We desire truth but find ourselves only in uncertainty." Karl Jaspers thought that the key question or philosophical problem was what it means to be human and what each person can become. The *Los Angeles Times Book Review* once opined: "The greatest mystery of all—What are we, exactly, and where do we come from?"

The more we seek to resolve these mysteries, the more intelligently and deeply we live. We know this in our hearts. Polymath Samuel Johnson said, "Curiosity is, among great and generous minds, the first passion and the last." There is no end to knowledge and true learning. Historian Daniel Boorstin called the human animal the "asking animal." Our instinct to question everything is what drives us to grow and thrive. Socrates famously said that the unexamined life is not worth living. All too easily, however, we can become distracted, scared, frustrated, gullible, cynical, or just plain inattentive. We suppress our natural questing spirit. We plow ahead without taking a good, hard look at what we're doing and why. And whether we realize it or not, we buy into ready-made systems of thought, habit, and belief sold to us by our culture, families, friends, and associates. We fall into step with the herd and almost unthinkingly adhere to whatever cult(ure) we're brought up in, unconsciously living out our received beliefs and assumptions, for the most part without question or examination.

But do we really have faith in these systems and our understanding as viewed through their lenses? Are they genuinely nourishing us as intelligent, discerning, warm-hearted souls? How well do they serve in today's world, when social, economic, political, and religious structures are in constant flux and so often can seem disconnected from our lives? How can we rekindle our questioning spirit's passionate curiosity, so that we can engage more dynamically in the grand adventure of life? How do we go about answering for ourselves the big questions that won't go away? How can we wonder about, rediscover, and plumb deeper into truth, reality, and understanding for ourselves—and even develop profound wisdom? Joseph Campbell says that different mythologies "give us the same essential quest. You leave the world that you're in and go into a depth or into a distance or up to a height. There you come to what was missing in your consciousness in the world you formerly inhabited." If the gods of antiquity are dead, who and what do we worship today?

The Big Questions explores a number of the most daunting and tantalizing questions each of us faces today. It will not give you final answers to these ultimate questions. Even more to the point, it will not provide *your* answers to these questions—the ones that resonate most strongly in your personal heart and your personal world. So why read it? Because it will help you learn to question more pointedly and deeply so you can respond to life's ultimate questions more wisely, effectively, and productively in your own reliable way. In short, it will engage you more actively in the holy curiosity at the heart of that sacred art of questioning.

The Big Questions draws heavily from my own personal questioning odyssey, one that led me as a young man to circumambulate the globe more than three times seeking guidance from many of the great gurus of our era, both Eastern and Western. It also taps into what I've learned over the past twenty years as a full-time teacher of Buddhism. In addition, it models the soul-searching efforts of many other individuals who collectively represent many different lifestyles, spiritual traditions, and schools of thought. I wrote this book with three main purposes in mind:

- To illuminate how questioning is a wisdom practice that leads directly to discovering for ourselves the wisdom, conviction, and inner certainty that lead to greater knowledge and understanding of the deepest issues and mysteries of life.

- To articulate major questions common to people throughout the ages as part of our true "higher" education and spiritual literacy: educating for living a meaningful life, not just education for making a living.

- To help provoke further self-inquiry aimed toward articulating our own, most personally vital question. This question calls to us and pulls us forward and simultaneously drives our dreams, ambitions, and desires, pushing us beyond our habitual limits and frameworks as we continue to consciously evolve towards a far more wise and intelligent future.

The art of questioning is a wisdom practice and, perhaps, the quintessential element in all wisdom practices. As humorist James Thurber has said, "It is better to know some of the questions than all the answers." Sometimes just listening to someone's question is enough to help them inch farther on their path of discovery. As you progress through the book and grow attuned to this practice of inquiry, you'll become increasingly more aware of not only the particular questions you're most compelled to address in your own life, but also cognizant of the teachers, resources, traditions, and methods that are most likely to steer you in a most rewarding direction. You'll also grow more confident in your own potential as a quester, a truth-seeker, a truth-knower, and a truth-teller. Seekers must one day become finders.

Thinking of this awareness training carries me back to my childhood. When I posed questions to my Dad, an intelligent and well-read man, he was always there for me. He took me out on the lawn of our suburban corner house in Long Island to look up at the stars and learn the constellations. He taught me to fish and play baseball and basketball. But as I got older, he used to answer my questions more and more often by saying,

"Look it up, Jeffrey. Tell me what you find out." (He is no longer alive, but if he were, wouldn't he enjoy today's far-reaching search engines?) In my little-boy mind, I nicknamed him "Look-It-Up Dad." I was amazed at how much I could find on my own by simply opening a map or atlas, dictionary, encyclopedia, or operating manual, or visiting the library. Probably that was the first inkling I had of my need to learn to think for myself and of my own genuine ability to do so.

I was well endowed with the Why Chromosome, incessantly pestering my teachers and parents with questions. Later I realized that all children have these questions. It's as if a receiving antennae protrudes from every pore of their bodies, like invisible little sensors receiving e-mail (in this case, energy-mail) from every part of the universe. The questions are outside calling to them, and yet inside, motivating them, as well. Questioning and answering are much more interwoven than we think—not unlike breathing in and breathing out. Can't we say as adults that questions are not only calling us forward to look at the world around us, but also directing us to look deeper inside ourselves? Joseph Campbell pointed to this truth in his well-known statement, "The big question is whether you are going to be able to say a hearty 'yes!' to your adventure."

Even now, life is asking you, me, and everyone a Big Question. In whatever particular form it appears to you personally, it is up to you to look deeply within yourself to hear and articulate it in order to improve the human interconnection we all share. It is through the ongoing personal process of undertaking this kind of larger existential quest that life's most pragmatic problems and issues are clarified and illumined. Are we up to the challenge, the quest—the search for truth and meaning, God, reality, fulfillment, and the secret of life? Everyone is called, but few choose to respond wholeheartedly, because it requires fearlessly facing serious doubts and living with them for a while. In overcoming this fear, we can all draw inspiration from these words of seminal Swiss psychologist Carl Jung: "Thinking people welcome doubt: It serves them as a valuable stepping stone to better knowledge."

Wherever and however you make your quest, you may discover that final answers to the big questions of life are still elusive, but you'll doubtless be able to deal with these questions much more effectively. I like the way Rabbi Michael Lerner addressed this issue. Someone once asked him why God allowed so many terrible and unfair things to happen in the world. He replied, "I want to start with the fact that I don't know, that there is a limitation of knowledge and understanding built into being a human being at this stage in the development of the consciousness of the universe . . . Having said that, I want to consider several lines of possible response, as long as you understand that I know these are not answers but only responses . . . The difference is this: an answer seeks to dissolve the question, a response recognizes the ongoing validity of the question and seeks to remain in connection with it."

From a Buddhist perspective, I see the fact that we're often troubled by so many questions lacking final answers as an aspect of our singular heritage as human beings. Doubt, skepticism, and dissatisfaction can be precipitating forces, not just hindrances. They can propel us into wider exploration and deeper inquiry than we might otherwise make. As psychoanalyst and author James Hollis says, "Doubt is a profound and effective spiritual motivator. Without doubt, no truism is transcended, no new knowledge found, no expansion of the imagination possible. Doubt is unsettling to the ego and those who are drawn to ideologies that promise the dispelling of doubt by preferring certainties will never grow." Dissatisfaction is our way of experiencing the threshold of questioning, seeking, and aspiring. The writer Barry Lopez tells us, "One must live in the middle of contradiction, because if all contradiction were eliminated at once, life would collapse. There are simply no definitive answers to some of the great pressing questions. You continue to live them out, making your life a worthy expression of leaning into the light." Without such dissatisfaction and uncertainty, what would fuel our quest for enlightenment? And without that quest, what would human life be worth?

How shall I live my life? Why are we here? Where did we/I come from, and where are we going? What happens when we die? Why do bad things happen to good people? Aren't these the bigger, more pertinent, genuinely heartfelt questions we all have to confront, at least at some point in our magical and mysterious lives? Jung said, "The most important question to ask about any dream is 'Why this dream now?'" I think this is a good question to ask regarding anything that happens to us.

Why this now? What does it mean/signify/indicate? How is this *connected*? In his *Journey without Goal*, Buddhist pioneer Chögyam Trungpa Rinpoche writes: "We need to encourage an attitude of constant questioning, which is a genuine part of our potential as students. If students were required to drop their questions, that would create armies of zombies—rows of jelly-fish . . . The questioning mind is absolutely necessary."

Long ago I concluded that Gautama Buddha understood nature and the interconnected workings of our inner world better than any other philosopher or religious founder. The enlightened Buddha constantly used questions as a way of help-ing people get to the bottom, or truth, of things. Rather than providing creeds and dogmas, he often led his interlocutors through a series of queries until they arrived at some valid con-clusions for themselves. Buddha famously pronounced fourteen questions he would not answer, stating that they were "uncon-ducive to realizing the enlightenment which I teach as the ulti-mate goal of spiritual life." These questions included Where does the world come from; where do the world and time and space end; and other such speculative inquiries. I find it inter-esting and encouraging to note that, unlike some fatuous know-it-alls, even an enlightened sage like the historical teacher called The Buddha did not pretend to have all the answers, but emphasized those of particular relevance to his particular enlightenment-quest.

Your own quest for meaning may take an entirely different direction from mine and leave you similarly indebted to other fonts of timeless wisdom. The important thing is not necessarily that you follow one particular path, but that you persevere in the journey, so that you can live a more joyous, fulfilled, and enlightened life. Socrates thought that understanding the perspectives of others on six great questions would help him become a more excellent human being. He asked: What is virtue? What is courage? What is justice? What is piety? What is moderation? What is good? The Socratic Method famously used questioning as the principle tool for acquiring self-knowledge as wisdom. "Know thyself," he constantly exhorted his pupils.

The questions you'll confront in this book were carefully chosen to stimulate and deepen inquiries into a wide variety of issues: age-old and contemporary, global and personal, spiritual and pragmatic. Obviously there isn't space here—or, for that matter, in any book—to address all of life's big questions. In addition, each person is almost certain to have a different assessment of the relative bigness of any one question based on his or her unique experience and situation.

I like to employ the question "Is it true?" when I hear or read about current concerns. Contemporary spiritual teacher Byron Katie's entire work centers around a very small number of basic questions. Katie asks people to apply her four Big Questions to their own issues, problems, concepts, and personal story lines: Is it true? Can you absolutely know it's true? How do you react when you think that thought? Who would you be without the thought? Katie's entire work and the basis of her mission revolve around asking these four big questions again and again. "I don't let go of the concepts, I question them," she says. "Then they let go of me."

Everyone has his or her own Big Questions, in one form or another. I was driving today and saw a bumper sticker that revealed one of the driver's Big Questions: "Why am I the only one on the planet who knows how to drive?" I am afraid it is going to be a long road for that seeker till he finds peace. I was thinking I might honk in solidarity with him, but he just drove off without even glancing my way!

If I were to be totally candid—and I hesitate to be honestly self-revelatory even here in private with you, dear reader—I'd have to say that my vital basic core question or issue is, "Why am I so rarely, if ever, satisfied, content, or fulfilled, and, if so, never for very long?" Perhaps that's why at the age of 20 I adopted Buddhism, which is based on the entire life problem of dissatisfaction and suffering; rooted in overweening desire and attachment and ceasing only in the deathless bliss and serenity of enlightenment or nirvana. How can I lead a happy, fulfilling, meaningful, useful life and leave the world a better place when I'm gone? My practical koan (or Zen conundrum) for clarifying daily action and intent is, What is the best thing I can do now in the present situation?

While I was peacefully lying on my friendly Buddhist chiropractor Tom Alden's table, I happened to ask him what his Big Questions were. He was quite forthcoming. "I have always had three questions which have helped me shape my life and grow," he said, while working on my lower back. "They are: What do I want? Whom or what do I trust? What do I love?" And then there are the big questions of our animal friends. My dog Lili, as always, wants to get into the act. Her BQ seems to be, "Why do you eat so often when I don't?" Albert Einstein expressed his Big Question as follows: "I want to know how God created this world. I am not interested in this or that phenomena, in the spectrum of this or that element. I want to know God's thoughts, the rest are details." Skye, the son of spiritual writer Anne Cushman, laboriously typed into Google the question: "Why do people kill other people?" when he was just learning to read and write. Alice B. Toklas, in a letter about Gertrude Stein's last deathbed words, writes, "She said upon waking from a sleep—'What is the question?' And I didn't answer, thinking she was not completely awake. Then she said again—'What is the question?' And before I could speak she went on—'If there is no question then there is no answer.'"

Perhaps you remember your first identity crisis and the teenager's age-old lament, "Why doesn't anyone understand and appreciate me?" Over an ice cream sundae, my teenage god-daughter, Patricia Duggan, touched me deeply by coming up with her big question, "Why are the things I love always being taken away?" I found this a pretty insightful and plaintive cry about loss and change from a 17-year-old high school senior. Recently, when I told her I was putting her BQ into the intro to my book, she commented wryly—a college freshman now—"It was nothing deep. When you asked if I had a big life question, I was just thinking about the strawberry shortcake sundae they used to have on the menu but was no longer there—not about my grandma's death or anything profound!"

Spiritual teacher Deepak Chopra states that the Big Questions revolve around Who am I? How do I fit in? What is the nature of good and evil? How do I find God? What's my life challenge? What is my greatest strength? What is my greatest struggle? What is my greatest temptation? Paulo Coelho, a Roman Catholic believer from Brazil and best-selling author of *The Alchemist,* said, "I know we all have the same questions. But we don't have the same answers." One of my favorite theologians, Paul Tillich, raised these three big questions:

- What is wrong with us? With men? Women? Society? What is the nature of alienation? Our dis-ease?

- What would we be like if we were whole? Healed? Actualized? If our potentiality was fulfilled?

- How do we move from the poor condition of brokenness to wholeness? What are the means of healing?

I hope this book will inspire you to identify and refine the questions that most concern you, whether or not they are directly addressed in this book. Many people have difficulty crystallizing their doubts, confusions, and vague longings into question form. Maybe you're one of them. Perhaps you put too much pressure on yourself to do things perfectly, and so you're reluctant to tread ambiguous waters, preferring simple material solutions or black-and-white certainties. Possibly you're afraid of what you may discover, or of failing at this great adventure of truth-seeking. Many people are out of touch with defining their innermost questions because society has conditioned them not to give in to their feelings or intuitions and not to dwell too much on mysteries or doubts. This book aims toward assisting you to do what the German poet Rainer Maria Rilke called "living in the question" rather than avoiding it, getting stuck in it, or settling for a fast, easy answer. This implies cultivating more tolerance for simply not knowing and for abiding in ambiguity, at least for a while, rather than hastily opting for the security and comfort of easy fixes via the certitudes of others.

As far as the questioning process is concerned, each life has its own best inner direction. As I've already indicated, the Buddha himself had two questions, which have formed the basis of the Buddhist path—the quest for enlightenment—for millennia. They are: What is the nature of suffering and its cause? and What are the practical steps to the end of suffering? These two questions, to which he responds in his renowned Four Noble Truths, can act like a healing modality, with those two basic questions functioning respectively as the diagnosis and the cure.

If I hadn't encountered Buddhism, I don't know what I would have done. Perhaps I'd be dead by now. Plenty of people in my generation, including some of my own close friends, did bite the dust early, due to the Vietnam War, drugs, motorcycle rides, thrill-seeking, or suicide. At college, where I was part of the anti-Vietnam War peace movement, I wondered how I was going to make a positive contribution to the world. I pondered whether being a writer, a therapist, or community activist, for example, would make the kind of difference that I felt was needed, and whether or not I had it in me to take on such a role. It was this kind of self-inquiry that eventually fueled my spiritual growth quest. I remember telling my roommate David when I left college that I was off to seek truth and reality, whatever that might mean. I was driven by a late-teen vision of what I thought of as Meister Eckhart's formless God. It would take me a decade and numerous discussions in India and Nepal with my Tibetan and Hindu yoga gurus to understand this vision.

During those years I explored the nature of society, the universe, and the mind through all kinds of reading, experiences, drugs, elders, lovers, and consciousness-raising practices, including fasting, chanting, yoga, encounter groups, Gestalt psychology, Eastern philosophy, Zen meditation, poetry and journal writing, Jungian dreamwork, mountain climbing and vision-questing. All of these endeavors helped me along my spiritual path and to find answers to the existential questions plaguing me.

As I set out to write this book, my extensive Big-Question polls of my students, colleagues, family, and friends confirmed the truth that everyone has their own list of life's big questions, although all of them circle around a few significant ones, including those about death and the afterworld, God, love, truth, suffering, good and evil, and reality. Sometimes a vital concern to one person is a trivial matter to another, and vice versa. I also want to make it clear that the order of the questions in this book is in no way indicative of the relative importance of the individual questions. My purpose here is to point the way for you to engage more wholeheartedly in your own questing. It's the grandest adventure life offers, a meaningful spiritual practice, and an extraordinary method of leaning into the light.

When it comes to the practical art of questioning and the practice of authentic, no-holds-barred self-inquiry, realizing your own most vital, genuine, core question is crucially important. What burning question is driving you in your quest, dreams, hopes, desires, and ambitions? Don't just tell me you want to know whether the stock market is going to go up or not, or who will win the next election or World Series; rather, trace back to the source of those small questions. Why do you want the market to go up? Why do you want to know that tiny piece of future information? What do you hope to get out of such tiny bits of foreknowledge, should they even be attainable? What do you hope to get out of the profits after obtaining them? Happiness? Comfort? Leisure? Success? Peace of mind? Security? Power? What do you expect those to bring you? What are you really after, beneath it all, beneath those time-bound worldly desires? What is it you seek, want, need, long for the most? Can you come up with your own volcanic question that's burning your bottom and constantly gnawing at your innards? This is *the* big question.

LAMA SURYA DAS
Cambridge, MA

Happiness cannot come from without. It must come from
within. It is not what we see and touch or that which others do
for us which makes us happy; it is that which we think and feel
and do, first for the other fellow and then for ourselves.

—HELEN KELLER

The time to be happy is now,
The place to be happy is here,
The way to be happy is to make others so.

—ROBERT INGERSOLL, 1842–1910

What Is Happiness and Where Can It Be Found?

In the early 1970s, thousands of spiritual pilgrims gathered to hear the Dalai Lama. He spoke in Bodh Gaya, India, near the Bodhi Tree where the historical Buddha experienced enlightenment 2,500 years ago. I was among them—a 21-year-old hippie who had taken the Overland Route from Europe through Turkey and Iran to Nepal. At the end of the Dalai Lama's talk, another longhaired American traveler asked him, "What is the meaning of life?" The Dalai Lama instantly responded, "To be happy and to make others happy."

Frankly, I was disappointed. My college philosophy courses

had led me to expect something more intellectual, recondite, or at least poetic. Wasn't that answer too facile? And isn't mere happiness a hedonistic, shallow, self-centered concern? After years of pondering that answer, I fully appreciated how profound it actually was. Yes, it sounds simple—just be happy and make others happy—but that doesn't mean it's easy to put into practice. How consistently are we able to think and act in ways that genuinely make us happy and that also make others happy? How is it even possible to have that kind of contentment, satisfaction, and mastery over our lives?

I'm not talking about maintaining surface-level happiness, like always wearing a smile or being a people-pleaser by constantly doing whatever others ask us to do. What I'm referring to goes much, much deeper. How often do we look for happiness by trying to escape from responsibility, by pursuing sensory gratification, or even by cultivating numbness (as in "feeling no pain")? In fact, these very endeavors wind up causing us grief in the end. I think of happiness as a deeply felt sense of joy and well-being, flourishing within a balanced, stable, integrated heart and mind. Aristotle called happiness "the only goal we choose for its own sake and never as a means to something else." Happiness may generally be thought of as a good feeling, but it also evolves from an attitude or way of choosing—consciously or unconsciously—how we view, interpret, and thus experience the world.

A wise elder I know said that happiness is love—loving all of life, just as it is, while working to tweak it just a bit as needed.

I have often said that happiness is contentment and acceptance, which is perhaps a little one-sided. Antoine de Saint-Exupéry, the author of the classic *The Little Prince*, said, "True happiness comes from the joy of deeds well done, the zest of creating things new."

A Tibetan lama once told me that the main problem with worldly people is that they are constantly seeking happiness and fulfillment outside themselves, where it cannot be found. Epicurus thought that a beautiful, righteous, and wise life was both the cause and the product of happiness. Plato famously said that the happiest man was the one who had no malice in his soul. Buddha himself further outlined what he called the five kinds of happiness:

- The happiness of the sense of pleasure

- The happiness from giving and sharing, including both external virtuous acts and inner mental states and attitudes

- The happiness, inner peace, and bliss arising from intensely concentrated states of meditative consciousness concomitant with purity of mind

- The happiness and fulfillment coming from insightful wisdom and profound understanding

- Nirvanic happiness, everlasting bliss and contentment, serenity, beatitude, and oneness

According to Buddhist positive psychology, happiness is part of our natural state, only obscured by attachments that veil our radiant, innate nature and limit our potential. The Hevajra Tantra teaches, "We are all Buddhas by nature; it is only adventitious obscurations which veil that fact." What we seek, we are. It is all within. This is the Buddha's secret.

Research in the emerging field of positive psychology—focusing on one's inner strengths and potential rather than on one's outer failures and problems—has shown that learned optimism and flexibility contribute a great deal to resetting happiness levels that have been compromised by genetic inheritance, personal biochemistry, social conditioning, and individual life experiences. This finding conflicts with what many scientists previously thought and confirms what yogis and other serious meditators have always known: We have an innate capacity to be happy that is independent from what happens to us.

The so-called happiness quotient (satisfaction level) and the genetic and socialized set-point for our mood carburetor (or emotional thermostat) can apparently be reset. When mood is positively shifted through intentional mental training, usually associated with mindfulness, compassion-development, and concentration exercises, the brain's left neo-cortex, involved in positive emotion, is boosted.

Part of the Buddhist practice of meditation is to awaken the mind to the fresh immediacy and preciousness of each moment. I know this can sound rather mystical and impractical to people who have never tried meditation, but recent scientific studies have also proved that, yes, meditators do tend to be happier people. Researchers at the University of Wisconsin studied the brainwaves of regular Buddhist meditators and found an unusual amount of electromagnetic activity in the prefrontal lobe areas linked to positive mind states. Researcher Fleet Maul, founder and president of Prison Dharma Network said, "Usually when we use the word 'happiness,' it refers to how we feel when things appear to be going our way. This kind of happiness is superficial and ultimately unsatisfying. During the 14 years I served in a maximum-security federal prison, it was clear that things did not appear to be going my way. Practicing the Buddhist path, grounded in meditation, study, precepts, practice, and service, I discovered an abiding cheerfulness and joy. This kind of happiness is worth pursuing."

My old friend Matthieu Ricard writes in his book, *Happiness: A Guide to Developing Life's Most Important Skill*, "I have come to understand that although some people are naturally happier than others, their happiness is still vulnerable and incomplete, and that achieving durable happiness as a way of being is a skill. It requires sustained effort in training the mind and developing a set of human qualities, such as inner peace, mindfulness, and altruistic love." I have often heard the Dalai Lama speak about altruism as the answer to our ills, because so much of the world's suffering and misery—both at the individual and collective levels—can be traced to greed, hatred, fear, and other negative qualities stemming from egotism and selfishness. Once he said, "If you want others to be happy, practice compassion. If you want to be happy, practice compassion." *The Art of Happiness: A Handbook for Living* was a groundbreaking collaboration between the Dalai Lama and the psychiatrist Howard C. Cutler, M.D. In this book, they maintain that happy people are generally found to be more sociable, flexible, creative, successful in mating, and better parents, able to tolerate life's daily frustrations more easily than unhappy people. And, most important, they are found to be more loving and forgiving than unhappy people.

Like the Dalai Lama and the Buddha himself, many modern scientists and philosophers agree that serving others is the secret to happiness, fulfillment, and a good and beautiful life. Others, however, posit that selfishness is a biological, evolutionary imperative, part and parcel of our survival mechanism. They say that altruism offers no added value or demonstrable advantages to our state as human beings, but is merely a faith-based practice. Whom shall we believe? Can we not find out for ourselves, in the inner laboratory of our own hearts and minds, through close scrutiny, trial and error, and our own experience? What I have noticed over the years is that the fewer selfish preoccupations I have and the more connected and thus less separate or boundaried I feel, the better things seem to go for me and the more I find in common with others.

One lama I know was recently dubbed the "happiest person in the world" by our trustworthy media, due to his outstanding performance on neuroscience tests (at the Mayo Clinic research labs), where he performed 700 to 800 percent higher on the scale than the average person—or even the average meditator—

when it came to intentionally producing good feelings through deliberate mental meditative concentrations revolving around common Tibetan Buddhist compassion and altruistic loving-kindness practices. The Bodhisattva exemplar of India, the 8th-century PeaceMaster Shantideva, said, "Happiness in this world comes from thinking less about ourselves and more about the well-being of others. Unhappiness comes from being preoccupied with the self." For millennia this age-old altruistic thought has been a Buddhist touchstone in the quest for happiness and satisfaction.

Some of us look at our possessions as sources of happiness. By possessions, I mean not only our material wealth but also our role in life, our status, and our public self-image. Our consumer society fuels and feeds on this kind of misplaced value system. It manipulates us to desire ever more wealth and popularity. Ubiquitous commercials even supply us with happiness behavior modeling: actors who demonstrate the joyful mannerisms we are supposed to display when we use a certain product or attain a particular status. What they don't show is all the unhappiness that can so easily come when we adopt these fantasy images as serious goals and they fail to deliver. We often hear this kind of unhappiness jokingly referred to as an illness: "Oh, she's got a bad case of affluenza!" or "I'm afraid he's suffering from hipatitis—you know, the terminal desire to be cool." The nervous laughter, however, masks a deep inner concern: Why aren't more people happy with these things? Why can't I be happy with these things? If these things don't bring happiness, then what does? Henny Youngman, an old-school Catskills comedian, said: "What's the use of happiness? It can't buy you money." Happiness can't be bought, but the fact that statistics reveal that shopping is America's favorite pastime seems to indicate that we mistakenly believe it can be.

We may think that getting what we want or having things go our way is the answer, but that does not necessarily turn out to be the case, either. My student Shana, for example, admits that she associates happiness, in part, with not having to work. When she takes a day or even a week off from her public relations job, she feels relieved and enjoys, at least intermittently, the novelty of the experience, the absence of specific pressures from her workload, colleagues, and clients, and the greater freedom she experiences with no appointment schedule. Meanwhile, she also feels slightly disoriented and still somewhat anxious about what's going on in her work world, although she usually manages to discount these feelings. She has committed herself to the point of view that a vacation is essentially a way to be happy, and her work, although financially necessary and occasionally rewarding in other ways, is essentially *not* a source of happiness. As a result, her vacation life is never quite as much fun as she'd expected and leaves her ultimately unsatisfied, because she dreads going back to the office again afterwards. Meanwhile, her work life becomes even more identified as a problem and even less able to give her a sense of accomplishment.

Shana's situation illustrates that we are not really very good at predicting what will make us happy or unhappy in any definite way. Instead, we seem to wander around searching, inevitably reliving the same old dualistic dramas: pleasure and pain, loss and gain, fame and shame, praise and criticism. Buddhists call them the Eight Worldly Pitfalls. It is not exactly that we can't or shouldn't enjoy things in the outside world. It's more a question of how attached we become to the world's impermanent, unreliable, and dreamlike phenomena. The more we associate them with happiness, the more they're bound to make us unhappy sooner or later. Samuel Johnson wrote: "The fountain of content must spring up in the mind, and he who hath so little knowledge of human nature as to seek happiness by changing anything but his own disposition, will waste his life in fruitless efforts and multiply the grief he proposes to remove."

Although research reports that most people say they are happy most of the time, annual antidepressant sales top 80 billion dollars in the United States. Meanwhile, in a Buddhist counterpoint: The tiny Buddhist kingdom of Bhutan has placed happiness at the top of the agenda, with the king announcing that prosperity is measured in Gross National Happiness rather than Gross National Product.

According to the World Database of Happiness in Nations Rank Report 2004, the most satisfied nations on Earth are, from the top: Switzerland, Malta, Denmark, Ireland, Iceland, Netherlands, Luxembourg, Canada, Finland, Sweden, New Zealand, and the USA. Feelings of happiness and satisfaction are more prevalent in countries with greater resources and basic necessities, personal freedoms, security, peace, education, social involvement, and so forth. According to researchers, if you want to raise your level of happiness by changing the external circumstances of your life, you should do the following: live in a wealthy democracy, get married, avoid negative events and negative emotions, acquire a rich social network, and get religion. Making more money, staying healthy, getting as much education as possible, changing your race through subterfuge or intermarriage, or moving to a sunnier climate have no overall statistical beneficial effect. People who cohabitate with others are more likely to report happiness than those who live alone, as are children in intact families and adults with health, paying work, and active lives. Often enough, retirement does not seem to bring people the happiness and contentment they once imagined. Little statistical correlation has been shown—ten to fifteen percent—between wealth, health, beauty, and happiness.

Some people become attached to a particular method of finding happiness because it once brought them a special kind of ecstatic (literally, "standing outside") pleasure. This is how hardcore addictions are built: The happiness-junkie returns again and again to the food, drink, dope, gambling habit, mindless TV viewing, reckless behavior, or abusive lover that once seemed to deliver exactly what he or she wanted. After habituation, the same satisfaction no longer comes, but the junkie can't stop thinking that it just might the next time. Sadly, the odds are woefully not in his or her favor.

The hopelessness of the situation reminds me of a Taoist teaching tale about a young boy who had always dreamed of hunting for rabbits and was finally allowed to do so for the first time. He took several weapons with him—a bow and arrow, a sling, a spear—but he wasn't really sure how to use them. Finally he caught sight of a rabbit a short distance ahead and chased after it. He wasn't gaining any ground and despaired of catching it. Then, all of a sudden, a tree fell on the rabbit and killed it. Thereafter, whenever the boy went rabbit hunting, he only took a hatchet and waited behind a tree for a rabbit to come along. Needless to say, he did not turn out to be a happily successful bunny hunter!

The Buddha warned against overweening attachment to transitory things or to people, which becomes a source of suffering rather than happiness. In particular, he cautioned against attaching to the notion of a separate, independent self that deserves "its own" happiness. How readily do we associate happiness with our personal self-interest, ignoring the fact that we are all deeply interconnected and interdependent? When we are genuinely connected, we find inexpressible love and fulfillment. Then we naturally and spontaneously communicate happiness and joyous fulfillment to the people around us, and that helps them do the same for the people in their world, and so on, in concentric circles radiating outwards from the awakened heart of happiness within us. And we can't be genuinely happy unless this kind of energy exchange is involved. The Buddha said in the Dhammapada (Wise Sayings), "If you speak or act with a calm, bright heart, then happiness follows you, like a shadow that never leaves."

How do we find such happiness? How do we break through the thoughts and activities we've come to associate with happiness that, in fact, fail to bring any form of lasting happiness, free from self-destructive conflicts?

For every individual, the path of discovery will be slightly different. This is not because happiness is a selfish pursuit, but, rather, because each of us needs to work through a uniquely different complex of experiences, conditionings, and expectations that block our path. I have been thinking that the crux of the happiness matter for me is whether or not I am in the moment, in the flow, at one with whatever is happening and I am doing. Otherwise, I'm lost in worry, and anxiety about past and future, plagued by what Buddhist meditators call "comparing mind," comparing what *is* to other so-called possibilities. When I am in the moment, I am living in what is called the "fourth time," not past, not future, not just present, but deeply into the current moment, the holy now, the eternal instant.

Recently, I was leading a workshop for my Buddhist Dzogchen group in Portland, Oregon. It took place in a nice church. We broke for lunch at 12:30, and I told the participants to be back at 2:00. At 2:00 I was in our meeting room waiting for everyone to arrive when I heard music coming from the main chapel. I opened the door and looked around the corner of the corridor, where I saw someone practicing on the huge old organ in the traditional main hall of the church, a balconied, three-tiered sacred space with excellent acoustics, carved wooden paneled walls, shiny wooden pews, and stained glass windows with light pouring in. I went back to our meeting room to see if everyone had gathered. Our local sangha leader remarked that they were gathering slowly and I should wait and relax. There I sat with the door open so I could hear the gorgeous organ music. I noticed that I was waiting almost impatiently for my students to gather—grumpily grizzling under my breath, thinking, "Why didn't I give them two hours for lunch? I could still be outside on this shining day!" Then I instinctively found myself at a fork in the road between the high ground and the slippery downward slope of resistance and resentment. I realized I could choose to turn toward the high ground. I did not have to wait impatiently, but could choose to settle into the glorious sacred sounds of the moment, acknowledging that the powers-that-be were providing a splendid organ recital for me. Suddenly I was totally there, with it, waiting for nothing and no one, immediately immersed in the sacred sounds of the holy now without regard for past, present, or future. Time passed swiftly in that state of grace. When I was called to conduct the afternoon session, all was well, very well. In retrospect this reminded me that opting for happiness and contentment is a decision that we can make at any time and that needs to be continually remade at every turn. When we are sufficiently conscious and aware, we can consistently choose that fork leading to the high road.

Here's an activity you can do to change your habitual ways of thinking about happiness and give yourself a better sense of what it means to you right now, at the starting point in your quest. Take at least a few moments to answer each of the following questions as specifically as possible, preferably in written form so you can more easily review your responses:

1. When have I felt the happiest and most alive, and why? Think of at least three answers, then substitute the following words for "when" and do the same thing: Where? How? With whom?

2. What specific sights do I associate with happiness, and why? Think of at least three answers, then substitute the following words for "sights": Sounds? Smells? Tastes? Physical sensations? Emotional feelings?

3. Review all of your answers and note the *common* elements—things that are repeated and that fall into similar categories.

4. Review all of your answers and note the *variety* of elements—the different categories of things that are represented.

5. Savor more deeply the present moment through cultivating total presence and mental serenity; take a deep breath or two, calm and clear, and then relax, centering and smiling.

The purpose of this activity is to provide concrete images and categories that you can ponder and contemplate thoroughly, and even bring to your daily meditations. Then you can more effectively do the deeper work of asking yourself how *you* define happiness. Is it in terms of feeling alive? Feeling secure? Winning? Being right? Feeling free? Feeling whole and complete? Loving? Being loved? Feeling connected and belonging?

Are there any other terms or feelings that you can think of?

Focusing on the same images and categories, you can also consider whether or not the happiness you associate with them is lasting, repeatable, nourishing, sharable, or costly, problematic, and so on. (Other adjectives and intuitions are certain to occur to you as you continue this consciously self-scrutinizing activity.) How you can go about living a happier life will become clearer to you the more you pursue and live with these thoughts and reflections, and learn to act upon them as you come to grips with your true values, concerns and priorities.

I also recommend periods of simple meditation *without* thinking, to whatever extent is feasible. Consciously try to practice merely observing—through lucid mindfulness and letting be—the statements, ideas, feelings, memories, plans, and moods as they pass through the magic reflecting pool of your mind. Allow them to move along without attempting to hold on to them. Eventually this kind of nonconceptual awareness practice will help your internal chatter to settle down, so you can simply savor the moment you're in, however it happens to present itself, without judgment, evaluation, reaction, interference or distortion by projections and interpretations. Try doing this for a few minutes up to a half-hour, whenever you have the time, but especially when you're feeling unhappy, bothered, troubled, agitated, overwhelmed, or simply distracted and unable to concentrate.

So often we mistake movement for meaning, losing ourselves in habitual distractions to insulate us against gnawing inner feelings, including dissatisfaction, doubt, loneliness, boredom, or anxiety. Much of our unhappiness comes from an unstable heart and mind, from unconscious drives and desires, and from mentally living in the past or the future. Without appreciating reality as it is, we miss the radiant moment at hand. As long as we're preoccupied with our former traumas and triumphs, or our fears and dreams about what might happen down the road, or who said what to whom, it's very difficult to appreciate and cherish the intrinsically joyful gift of life right here, now.

I personally believe that happiness is our spiritual birthright. It's the counterpart to suffering, which, as the Buddha said, permeates life in the temporal world as long as we remain attached to worldly things and desires. An ancient Chinese saying advises, "If you want happiness for an hour, take a nap. If you want happiness for a day, go fishing. If you want happiness for a month, get married. If you want happiness for a year, inherit a fortune. If you want happiness for a lifetime, help someone else. If you want eternal happiness, know yourself." I'm convinced that the key to claiming our spiritual birthright lies in appreciating fully that we belong to something larger than our individual selves, something beyond any of us and yet immanent in each of us—far beyond our worldly personal desires.

In Buddhism, this awakened awareness is called realizing our Buddha nature. It allows us to participate wholeheartedly in joys that are universal—the specialness of each moment, the beauty of the natural world, the wondrous feelings that go with acts of kindness—rather than to grab coldheartedly at fleeting pleasures based on separating ourselves from others, like making more money, achieving fame, or seeking more thrills. We discover our proper fit in the world and why we're alive. Then buoyant happiness becomes an essential, permanent element in our state of being, and universal energy constantly flows through us.

This doesn't mean that we go around blissed-out all the time. We still experience sorrow, anger, grief, solemnity, but only in appropriate ways and at relevant times. Once the time for these emotions has passed, we don't cling to them and allow them to sink us into depression or irritability. Instead, our deep-seated happiness naturally returns. As the Zen master Thich Nhat Han says, "There is no way to happiness. Happiness is the way."

The most important thing is to find out what is the most important thing.

—ZEN MASTER SUZUKI ROSHI

What is the Meaning of Life and What is My Purpose Here?

The setting is usually a mountaintop, but sometimes simply a cave. An exhausted and distraught seeker, clearly at the end of a long, laborious journey, approaches a bald, bearded, and serene elder sitting in lotus position, wearing a plain white robe. Because this latter figure displays all the external signs of a wise teacher, the wayfarer asks the traditional question of questions: "What is the meaning of life?"

Most often we see this situation in the form of a cartoon, and the holy man's answer is something blatantly silly, like, "I wish I could tell you but my computer's down," or "First climb *every* mountain—then we'll talk!" Other times, we confront the big question about the meaning of life in a more serious context. For example, we may read about it in a Zen Buddhist collection of koans, or mind-stretching teaching encounters.

Asian Zen masters have traditionally answered their inquiring disciples with koans that may seem as absurd as the punch line of a cartoon, even though we're meant to accept these paradoxical utterances as fundamental truths. What is reality? What is wisdom? "It's the cypress tree in the garden," or "Look in the mirror;" "Sleep when tired, eat when hungry," or the ultimate nonduality as expressed in another scriptural story, when "His silence resounded like thunder." Singer John Cougar Mellencamp once titled an album, Nothin' Matters, and What If It Did? What does this tell us about the nature of this evergreen question about life's ultimate meaning? Why do we joke about it so much? Why do the wacky and profound responses sound so much alike? What is the real question within this timeless question about our mysterious, marvelous existence?

In September of 2006, I had the privilege of offering three lectures during the Dalai Lama's visit to my alma mater, The University at Buffalo, New York. In a meeting with the faculty during another part of that three-day visit, one of the professors stood up and asked the Lama, "Why are we born on this earth? Why are we here?" The Dalai Lama replied in English, with a chuckle: "Within theistic system, God knows. Ask him!"

I believe the question, "What is the meaning of life?" can't be answered in any definitive sense. Nor should it paralyze us with doubts and hesitation. I find that it's useful to keep the inquiry alive by recasting the question in various ways, year by year, day by day, moment by moment, to help keep our hearts open to the mystery and freshness of aliveness. I often wonder "What is this? What is happening, right here now?" and try to see, feel, and experience things objectively, calmly and clearly—just as they are, beyond interpretation. After an entire adult lifetime wrestling with these matters, I have arrived at the firm conclusion that the meaning of life is truly discovered only though living life and not according to any abstract formulation or master plan. The meaning of life is—now hear this!—exactly what we make of it and what we make it out to be: in other words, what we invest in it. You can take this answer to the bank.

The ancient Greek philosopher Epictetus said, "Man is troubled not by events, but by the meaning he gives to them." There's a part of the human psyche that wants a specific answer to everything—even, maybe especially, the ultimate puzzle: What is the meaning of life? Facing this age-old enigma, some people offer very general responses, like "Gain wisdom," "Serve God," "Be compassionate," or "Find love." These answers sound good, but they're still too abstract to satisfy our itch for the specific. There must be more to it than that, we insist. Surely the secret is more colorful, more dramatic, more mind-blowing! To be happy sounds simple, but it is not easy.

Carl Jung wrote in *Memories, Dreams, Reflections,* "Probably as in all metaphysical questions, both are true: Life is—or has—meaning and meaninglessness." Other great thinkers and teachers imply that there is no answer to the question, or that life has no fixed and particular meaning. Various Mahayana Buddhist texts tell us that the heart of life and the nature of the universe are inherently mysterious and unknowable. This is one interpretation of sunyata—the emptiness that pervades every form so that the two apparent opposites (emptiness and form) can't, in fact, be separated, and are understood as being complementary rather than contradictory. Does this mean that we live in a nihilistic universe? Are we really free to do whatever we want because nothing matters, life has no point?

The answer in both cases is no, precisely because the question of meaning keeps reasserting itself in our minds. Philosopher David Schmidtz reminds us that meanings change over time. If a deep meaning is possible, "maybe life per se is not the kind of thing that can have it. A deep, worthwhile life is simply a series of mostly worthwhile—sometimes deeply worthwhile—episodes." He asks, "Why would that not be enough?" What are we looking for? It is this questioning spirit that not only propels our lives forward, but also affirms that life itself does have meaning, according to how we live it. I'm reminded of a dialogue that occurred between Shunryu Suzuki, founder of the Zen Center of San Francisco, and one of his students. The student said, "I don't know what the first principle is." Suzuki responded, "I don't know *is* the first principle." Many

THE BIG QUESTIONS

times the answer to a question lies in the question itself, and no more so than here. Taking a lesson from Suzuki Roshi, we might do well to rephrase the question "What is the meaning of life?" to produce the answer, "'*What*?' is the meaning of life."

Wonder is an important part of life's secret, I believe. Child-like wonder, reverence, and awe help keep us from becoming jaded or dry intellectuals and remain truly alive. One Zen master I knew said that the purpose and aim of his life was to live every day and every moment with hope and joy, simply appreciating the extraordinariness of the ordinary.

Writer Henry Miller thought that "The aim of life is to live, and to live means to be aware, joyously, drunkenly, divinely aware." At the age of 80, after doctors informed him he should already be dead from kidney disease, prize-winning journalist Art Buchwald said that the two questions uppermost in his mind were "What am I doing here?" and "Where am I going?" He said that he knew he was put here on earth to make people laugh, but that the second question was much harder— he had no idea. Moreover, he felt that no one else knew the answer to the latter question, and if they said they did, they were talking through their hats.

We would do well to notice that there are various kinds and dimensions of meaning for various people. For some, the meaning of life is found in work, through career and accomplishments; for others, in love, family, and children; some find it most deeply through service to God or service to humankind. I am glad to see that altruism, volunteerism, and interconnectedness have recently come to the fore in public conversation about charity and the gross inequalities in both our society and in the greater world.

Dr. Martin Luther King, Jr., said, "An individual has not started living until he can rise above the narrow confines of his individualistic concerns to the broader concerns of humanity." Nobel Laureate Eli Wiesel writes, "If to be free is the most important goal of all, then to help someone to be free or become free must be the most sublime and rewarding of human endeavors."

Some say life has no real purpose or meaning, but I feel that is nonsense. I think what they really mean is that, *to them,* life does not seem to have a universal purpose for all of us, or they feel that life has become personally meaningless. I understand that feeling, but that does not necessarily imply that it matches reality.

Why is there anything at all rather than nothing? What is the nature of reality? There are various forms of the timeless meaning-of-life question. Not unlike spiritual seekers and philosophers, modern scientists too strive to unravel these questions.

Austrian psychiatrist Victor Frankl is reputed to have coined the term "Sunday Depression" in reference to the feelings of emptiness and lack of meaning many people feel at the end of their work week. Frankl survived the Holocaust in Nazi concentration camps, where he decided that all of humanity can be divided into two groups: decent and non-decent people. In his classic *Man's Search for Meaning*, he said that he thought "What is the meaning of life?" is not the right question. "[In the camps] . . . it did not really matter what we expected from life, but rather what life expected from us. We needed to stop asking about the meaning of life, and instead think of ourselves as those who were being questioned by life—daily and hourly." In the crucible of anguish during several years in those camps, he concluded that even suffering contains meaning and purpose, a profound insight which informed his own trauma therapy in the postwar decades.

At this point in my life, what is the meaning of life seems to me too as a slightly misleading question. The meaning of life must be discovered through living. Each of us must find our own meaning. Although we can claim the meaning ascribed by someone else—St. Paul, Mao, Billy Graham, Buddha—we still must live it out for ourselves and reap the genuine satisfactions and fulfillment, or lack of them, depending on our own authenticity. To find our own meaning and purpose of life, we must at some point inquire into certain questions. What is most meaningful to me? What do I care about the most? Who or what do I actually devote myself to? What is (my) life all about?

Our individual ways of thinking about these big questions, like all things we consider, depend on our almost entirely subjective frames of reference. Some seem to think that life is meaningless or absurd, even tragic; yet somehow they remain dedicated to someone or something. Some scientists say that the meaning and purpose of life is to reproduce so that the species can continue to evolve. From a religious point of view, meaning and purpose depend on your particular faith and affiliation. Buddhists might say the purpose or goal of life is enlightenment, nirvana—deathless bliss and peace. Christians might say it is to do God's work and to reach heaven, or to commune with God. The "Baltimore Catechism" states that the purpose of life is to know God and enjoy him endlessly. Humanists often tell me that the purpose of life is to be a genuinely good person, help others, and contribute to a better world.

Dr. Martin Luther King said, "An individual has not started living until he can rise above the narrow confines of his individualistic concerns to the broader concerns of humanity." Nobel Laureate Eli Wiesel writes: "If to be free is the most important goal of all, then to help someone to be free or become free must be the most sublime and rewarding of human endeavors." I personally agree with all of this, in general, while noticing that so many of us are eager to change the world, while relatively few are ready, willing, and able to change themselves in order to really help do so. Many are called, but few choose to awaken, become wise and experienced Elders, and strive together mightily towards transformative action.

One helpful approach to this big question about life's meaning and purpose is to take a good hard look at our lives and ask ourselves *where* we are looking for an answer. Are we depending upon someone else to answer it for us, such as a guru on the mountaintop, or some stone tablets, or holy scripture? Wouldn't it be great if that could happen? Or would it, considering the hazards, skills, and blind luck required to locate such a guru and get to that mountaintop? In fact, there are many people who no doubt can help guide us along the way to the truth, including people we already know, but we must discover that truth on our own if it's going to have any vital function in our lives. We must never confuse the teacher with the truth. To paraphrase an ancient Buddhist expression, we must not mistake the finger pointing to the moon for the moon itself.

Are we assuming that the truth exists in Tibet or some Holy Land or heavenly sphere rather than in our home town? Perhaps in a place of worship or a peaceful monastery, but not our own home? By definition, any universal truth can be realized anywhere. Are we conditioned to believe that the truth only appears to us when we're in a state of agony or ecstasy? We need to overcome the habit of seeing the truth as something that's esoteric, for elite spiritual Olympiads only, or only available to us under extreme conditions. Buddhism emphasizes living according to the Middle Way, a balanced way between extreme views and dogmatic beliefs. The doctrine arose from the historical Buddha's own life experience. As a totally pampered, self-indulgent young prince, he was unable to see the nitty-gritty realities and profundities of life, so he left his palace and became a wandering yogi. Despite denying himself food, clothing, or shelter almost to the point of death, he was just as unable to perceive any meaning in his life. He decided that the right way to realize the truth was to live midway between these two fundamentally distracting polarities—hedonistic worldliness on the one hand, or ascetic other-worldliness on the other. Not too much and not too little, neither too tight nor too loose: This is the wisdom way of balance and harmony.

In seeking the answer to the question we're considering here, I believe the solution lies in following this Middle Way—becoming neither a self-centered hedonist nor a self-denying ascetic. To walk this path, to stay in the middle without veering too far one way or the other, we must stay especially awake and alertly aware each moment. Perhaps this kind of mindfulness relates to the meaning of life. Another dimension of following the Middle Way in this quest to find the genuine meaning of life is to aim somewhere between getting a definite answer and tolerating the discomfiting experience of no answer at all. We need to learn how to live consciously and, trusting ourselves, purposefully on that inevitable balance point between form and emptiness, relative and absolute, being and non-being, self and non-self, time and eternity, the finite and infinity. It is between all such dichotomies and poles that our life actually flows.

After the general question, "What is the meaning of life?" come the specific questions, "What is *my* special purpose in life; why am I here?" It's important to consider the former question first, because it takes us beyond our individual self to the universe as a whole. After all, we are not isolated beings, separate from everything else. Much enters into our personal world about which we have no foreknowledge and over which we have no control. In turn, much in our personal world affects others in ways we can't imagine, predict, or influence. It's a challenge to allow this much mystery into our daily existence and yet simultaneously persist in seeking clarity and significance in life and the universe.

We are obliged to live as if there's meaning in life, without any guarantee that there is. In that endeavor lies all the glory, honor, wonder, and, yes, meaning of life. As the French philosopher André Gide said, "Believe those who are seeking the truth. Doubt those who find it."

Suppose we're not actively engaged in the search for life's meaning and our own special purpose and place in it all. Nevertheless, uncertainty about these issues can linger with us, sapping our energy and undermining our dreams and aspirations. It may go unnoticed for a while, possibly years; then, a sudden change in our own fortunes or in the world around us forces them to the surface again, and we agonize anew: "What is my purpose?" "Why was I born?" "Where do I fit into the scheme of things?" or even, more simply, the modern sitcom-like dilemma, "What am I gonna do now?" The only thing I can say with any conviction about these questions is that the answers are to be found in loving and being loved, in hope and patient forbearance, and in beginning each day anew. My constant daily question is, "What is the best thing I can do now in this situation, given these circumstances? Much is provided; now, what is required from me?"

Imagine if someone—or something—miraculously informed us during our teens or twenties about what our calling in life was to be. It would be like getting a kind of positive, spiritual draft notice that immediately made us realize, "Yes! Of course! This is what I was meant to do!" Wouldn't it be wonderful to know exactly where we needed to head in order to find fulfillment? Wouldn't it save us years of unnecessary confusion, mistakes, and wasted effort? Or would it carry its own price, bringing with it an entirely different but equally troublesome set of questions, like, "How am I going to do *that*?" "What if it brings hardship to me and my loved ones?" What happens if I fail?" And, as so often is the case in family businesses and inherited occupations, "Is this really for me?" Poet Mary Oliver poses: "Tell me what is it you plan to do with your one wild and precious life?"

Stories abound of people who receive clear, resonant messages from unimpeachable spiritual sources about their proper mission in life. God himself appeared in different forms to Moses, Jesus, and Mohammed while they were young and set them on course to becoming great religious leaders. In 15th-century France, Joan of Arc, the teenage leader of an army that placed Charles VII on the throne, apparently received her audacious marching orders directly from visions of St. Michael, St. Catherine, and St. Margaret. The 18th-century American adolescent John Chapman encountered a celestial being who told him to plant apple trees ahead of the pioneers settling the Ohio territory, and so he transformed himself into the person we now know as Johnny Appleseed.

For other people, the summons comes in a less dramatic form

and involves a less extreme, more practical way of living. In fact, the lucky recipient may not even recognize when the calling first manifested itself, except later in hindsight as he or she looks back to the beginning of a path well taken. Take Kelee Katillac, for example, the founder of a highly unusual and creative interior design business called House of Belief. She traces her calling back fourteen years to a time when she was poor, lived in a shabby trailer park in Kansas, and had no idea what to do with her life. One afternoon she spotted a broken-down chair by the side of the road. Some strange impulse made her take it home and spend weeks restoring it. As she said to reporter Kingsley Hammett in *Designer/Builder* magazine (July/August 2002), "I essentially applied what was left within me to that chair."

Inspired by this experience, Katillac redecorated her entire trailer, stamping it, too, with her own distinctive style. This act led to other jobs in the area, a position with a Kansas City interior design firm, and, eventually, to a lucrative freelance career in New York City. But her worldly success left her feeling jaded and unmotivated. Her wealthy clients preferred simply buying her designs without making any creative contribution of their own. Having realized her own personal dream, she hungered to help others realize theirs.

Katillac's intuition led her to return to her roots in Kansas City, where she felt most in touch with the people around her. There she created a revolutionary new decorating process: professional consultants help clients to achieve their own designs through a guided process. First the clients re-examine their core values, major interests, and favorite possessions. They tap memories of homes and environments they've enjoyed in the past. Finally, they learn how to translate their ideas for their resulting home interior designs into physical images, plans, and scale models. Responding to the practical needs of low-income Habitat for Humanity homeowners, Katillac has also adapted her client-based approach to include workshops in painting, sewing, and upholstery. These skill-building workshops have helped many poverty-level clients not only more beautifully furnish their dwellings, but also enter the marketplace with new skills.

Having a calling or meaningful and fulfilling purpose in life, however, does not necessarily mean being drawn to a certain kind of job, task, or professional mission. Many people are compelled instead to commit themselves to a particular set of values—ones that they infuse into every aspect of their life, regardless of the various roles they play or situations they address as they go through their daily lives. I count myself as a member of this latter group. Growing up, I wanted to be happy, of course, and to accomplish something meaningful, but I began to appreciate more and more that I couldn't possibly feel happy and serene for long if others around me were confused and miserable. Part of this realization came from my heart and part from my cultural conditioning. I was brought up in a loving Jewish household that gave me the ideal of being a *mensch*: a good guy, a mature person, a decent citizen who derives a sense of purpose in life from being useful to others, contributing to the community, and unselfishly helping to make the world a better place.

That calling led me eventually, if unexpectedly, to the Tibetan refugee monasteries of my teachers in Nepal and in Darjeeling. There, in 1972, I first formally took the Bodhisattva vow to edify and free all sentient beings. That journey may strike someone who doesn't know me as an exotic departure from my sports-filled suburban Long Island past, but to me it was a natural extension of my earliest teenage intuition of the absolute necessity of finding a meaningful and positive purpose in life.

Joan Didion recently penned a terrific memoir called *The Year of Magical Thinking*, written soon after the death of her husband and daughter. In it she says that as a child she thought a great deal about meaninglessness and eventually found solace in geology. It was a sense of the larger sweep of geological events and change that helped her realize her small yet vital place in life. Later she found meaning in the Episcopal litany's words: "As it was in the beginning, is now and ever shall be, world without end."

I believe we all live in this world for some reason. Buddhists would say that this reason has to do with karma. Fundamentally, karma is the law of cause and effect: Every action has a consequence that sets in motion the next action, and so on. Nothing happens by accident. We see karma at work throughout time and space—the world of samsara. It governs the formation of galaxies, as well as the evolution of a single life, a single mind, a single thought or feeling. Each thought we entertain, each word we express, each deed we do helps determine the direction in which our life is going to move. According to the Buddhist doctrine of rebirth, the tendency that one lifetime has taken as it comes to an end carries over into a subsequent lifetime. This is the process of karma, or causation through interdependence and interconnectedness.

Whether or not we subscribe to the doctrine of rebirth or confine our attention to just this lifetime, the main point is that we are predisposed toward conditioned ways of thinking, feeling, speaking, or behaving by what we've thought, said, or done in the past. The reason we're alive is to take responsibility for this fact and, in doing so, work toward making sure our lives head in a positive direction, toward the three jewels of compassion, wisdom, and enlightenment instead of the corresponding three poisons of greed, anger, and ignorance. When we take on this mission, magical things begin to happen. We see more clearly into our true spirit, our innate Buddha nature. We perceive it in others, as well, and are impelled toward more fulfilling and connected ways of existing.

Joseph Campbell, an eminent American authority on mythology and its relationship to psychology and our lives, described this process as "following your bliss" in order to realize your true purpose in life. Thanks to the consumer-oriented society in which we live, many of us mistakenly think of bliss as a kind of shallow, poolside ecstasy, in which we experience complete sensory satisfaction without a trace of worry or discomfort. The kind of bliss Campbell means goes much deeper. It refers to an inner well-being and completeness that arises from doing something that brings out the best in us, something that we authentically love doing, even if it entails harder work and more sacrifice than any other career we could undertake. Once we accept the truth of this approach, we can see the danger that lies in believing that our purpose in life must be a particular goal toward which we aim single-mindedly: an Olympic gold medal, a multi-million-dollar bank account, a cure for cancer, a star on Sunset Boulevard. The reason we are born is so that our own most perfect gift will emerge naturally in the world. We must trust this fact.

When interviewing the Dalai Lama, author Victor Chan asked, "You have been a Buddhist monk for all your life. Let's not talk about difficult things like nirvana or enlightenment. But what do you want to achieve?" To which the Dalai Lama replied: "To be happy. My practice helps me lead a useful life. If I can give some short moment of happiness to others, then I feel that my life has achieved some purpose. This gives me deep mental satisfaction—this feeling always comes if you serve others. So when I help others, I feel happy. For me, the most important thing is human compassion, a sense of caring for one another."

Here are key questions to ask in considering your purpose in life:

- What do I treasure most in life? What specific moments and images in my life do I associate with what I most treasure in life?

- What thoughts, words, and actions bring me closer in touch to what I treasure most in life? How can I increase the occurrence or impact of such thoughts, words, and actions?

- What thoughts, words, and deeds seem to separate me from what I most treasure in life? How can I decrease the occurrence or impact of such thoughts, words, and deeds?

- Who are my heroes: people who seem to have had a strong, admirable purpose in life? How do these heroes or their lives relate to positive aspects in my own character and life?

- Where am I headed now and how much do I care about that?

- How could I change the course of my life so that I'd be more devoted to the things that most meaningfully concern me in both the short- and long-term picture?

It is now or never, as always. Ask a real question, pursue an authentic line of inquiry, and unlock a new world.

Confucius said, "If a person doesn't say to himself 'What to do? What to do?' indeed, I do not know what to do with such a person!" Through periodic self-inquiry we can come to see more clearly and deeply the meaning of life and our purpose in it, moment by marvelous moment, day by sacred day.

3

Knowing the world is knowledge; knowing oneself is wisdom.
—LAO TSU IN *TAO TE CHING*

The question, "Who am I?" contains the answers to all the questions about the soul, God, and the afterlife.
—RABINDRANATH TAGORE

Who Am I?

In one of his movies, the comedian W.C. Fields walks into a bank and up to the teller's window. The teller asks, "Can you identify yourself?" Fields says, "Of course. Do you have a mirror?" When presented with one, Fields immediately states, "Yup, that's me!" It's meant as a joke, but it carries a ring of truth. Who among us can say they really know themselves, without illusions, beyond the face in the mirror, their name-rank-and-serial-number role in the world, their personas, defense mechanisms, and self-deceptions? Do we distinguish between when we are being authentic and inauthentic? Do we know what we really feel about things, what our true values and priorities are, what lies below the surface of consciousness, and what makes us tick?

The question of identity—that is, about existence and our place in it—is one of our biggest existential conundrums. Spiritual self-inquiry is the most incisive and direct tool for accessing the depths of insight and self-knowledge inherent in this deep question. German novelist Thomas Mann wrote: "Introspection is the first step towards transformation, and I understand that, after knowing himself, nobody can continue to be the same." Stephen King, author of over 40 novels, says, "The question which haunts and nags and won't completely let go is this one: Who am I when I write?"

We may not continuously be troubled by the question of our identity, but most, if not all, of us experience some kind of serious identity crisis when we are teenagers and again in middle age, as we struggle to come to terms with where we've been, where we are, and where we're going. It's natural and important to our development and should not be avoided, short-circuited, ignored, or medicated away. This process is where learning how to live with the questions rather than rushing towards easy answers becomes invaluable. When we work to resolve who we are, we can more meaningfully and intelligently choose what we want to do with our life. People have actually become enlightened by concentrating on the very question, "Who am I?" Thus the ancient Chinese Zen master Yen-tou said, "There is no other real task but to know your original nature. Just look into your heart-mind, and find there transcendental clarity. Free from greed or dependency, you will immediately attain certainty." Thus Carl Jung, one of the pioneers of modern psychology, said, "Who looks outside, dreams. Who looks inside, awakes." Ramana Maharshi, one of the greatest saints of India during the last century, taught that, "No one doubts that he exists, though they may doubt existence of God. If you find out the truth about yourself and discover your own source, that is all that is required."

Confronting the question "Who am I?" often seems absurd on some level. Why ask it at all, unless we're suffering from amnesia? Speaking on my own behalf, isn't it clear to me that I am Surya Das, Jeffrey Miller, a male American with a home in Massachusetts, a predilection for chocolate ice cream, and various other familiar habitual attributes, roles and relationships, possessions, preferences, proclivities, and responsibilities? To shore up the island of individual existence against the tides of existential emptiness, we reify ourselves, using our memory to create and continuously reinforce our self-image, our story, our gated and well-defended island-state. Indeed, we are constantly engaged in the self-construction business, on both outer and inner levels, through both thought and actions, in our ongoing effort to convince not only others but ourselves that we really exist. Much of what we do, especially in our earliest decades, is directed towards separating from mother, differentiating from parental figures, constructing an identity and self-image, and finding our own voice, work, and place in the world. Some of us even become a brand name, like Oprah, Madonna, Martha Stewart, or Donald Trump; yet none of this is truly real or lasting.

I'm not saying that that the self doesn't exist. What I'm saying is that it's not a fixed entity. It is more a swirling congeries of forces, a whirligig of habits and conditioning relating to body, mind, and spirit—not unlike everything else that is temporarily cobbled together in this impermanent world. From this fact comes the Buddha's notion of the relative, interdependent, contingent self as an ego-generated identity rather than something that has a solid core or soul unto itself. In this respect, the word *self* is as much a verb as a noun, for we are constantly selfing and re-selfing, in order to maintain our illusory separate existence. This leads to possessiveness, a sense of separation, fears of all kinds, and the clinging that co-arises with selfish, deluded, dualistic notions of me and mine.

"To self or not to self?" Perhaps this is the main question of life, not quite what Hamlet famously wondered. Without an egocentric agenda, when awareness is not self-referential, we experience infinite freedom, clarity, peace, and spontaneity, unmediated by subjective interference and interpretation, inhibition and fabrication. Naked reality is revealed before our transparent, naturally open mind in all its radiant, majestic splendor and mystery, just as it is. The magical, dream-like nature of things is still vividly present, yet we are no longer deceived by its transitory, if solid-seeming, nature.

The truth is that there's no end to the possible answers to genuinely profound questions: "Who am I?" "What is the nature of self and consciousness?" "What is the soul?" Accordingly, these questions have bedeviled human beings throughout history. It's as if there's something within us that can't help seeking a once-and-for-all, final statement on the matter. Individually we build word chains in an attempt to package our identity, like "I'm a Virgo, Type A, vegan, middle-management, non-smoker, narcissist . . ." and so on. Our word chains get reconfigured with each new habit we develop, system we learn, identity we cultivate, and life-stage we enter. But is this really the kind of self-knowledge classification that Socrates had in mind when he inscribed *Know Thyself*—a commandment that is often cited as the cornerstone of Western philosophy and civilization—above the door to his academy? Do these words even begin to describe the "I" that seeks a greater sense of belonging in the universe, the "I" or supreme Self that the great spiritual traditions address in their teachings?

Sometimes we attach ourselves so strongly to a particular role we play that we're able to completely dodge the question "Who am I?"—at least until that role changes or ends. One of the first times I remember seriously asking myself the question was when I entered adolescence. Physical developments alone were telling me I wasn't a child anymore, in the common sense of the word, and yet my continuing dependence on my parents didn't make me feel quite like a man. There was more to my wonderment than that, however. I also experienced a new depth and urgency in the way I thought and felt about things. I may not have been able to put it into words at the time, but I was becoming aware that I was more than just a living being called Jeffrey Miller, that the nature of who I was extended way beyond that, perhaps even everywhere. Many people experience this same kind of mystery about who they are when their marriage falls apart and they can no longer call themselves a spouse, or when they are downsized or retire from a challenging career, and the title, work, and persona-building reinforcement that go with the job and professional role suddenly ceasing.

Some of us avoid the question of who we really are by creating special identities for ourselves. We take up hobbies, buy products, dye our hair, decorate our rooms, join groups and form opinions that fit a certain image of who we want to be or who, we think, might be successful, secure, hip, or admired in the outside world.

To varying extents, when we do something that goes against our normal behavior or that contradicts our established image of ourselves, we question who we truly are. It can happen whenever we don't live up to a resolution we make; for example: "I will quit smoking," "I will pass my bar exam," "I will become a painter," or "I will take my family camping." It can also happen whenever we do something potentially positive but completely against the usual grain, such as taking a day off from urgent work simply to relax, or letting ourselves be talked into an assignment or chore we typically try to avoid.

All of these self-reassessment triggers give us a glimpse of how incomplete and relative our personal identity is. In fact, Buddhism teaches that the self as we know it doesn't exist as a fixed entity. Each of us is interconnected with everything else in the universe. The more we persist in thinking of ourselves as separate beings, inside what Zen Buddhism describes as our separate "skin bags," the more we constrict and delude ourselves and the more we invite suffering into our lives.

So if the self isn't a fixed entity, why do we develop such a strong "sense of self?" In the world of everyday life, we need to have *some* concept of self simply to cross the street without getting hit by a car, let alone earn a living or raise a family. The key point is to realize that this abstract concept is just that— only a convenient fiction for helping us navigate through the real world, what Buddhism calls the realm of samsara (or bondage to worldliness) as opposed to the realm of nirvana, which is blissful peace, harmony, and freedom.

From the Buddhist point of view, the truth is that what we call the self is only a bundle of aggregates that constantly shift. Each of us is more than all of these aggregates put together. Each of us experiences and reflects all humanity, as well as the universe. And each of us is experienced and reflected by that same universe. The Buddha wanted human beings to realize their fundamental Buddha nature—the inherent, self-transcendent perfection they have in common with everything else in the universe. Buddhism thinks of the self as an illusory but functional bundle of parts interconnected with everything else, rather than a separate, permanent essence or eternal soul.

Even the most tangible part of ourselves, our physical body, changes all of the time. Do we look the same way we did 5 or 10 or 20 years ago? According to urban legend, over a period of seven years every cell in the body is completely replaced. Meanwhile, our mind exists in a constant state of flux, with ever-turning thoughts and emotions. So ask yourself again, "Who am I? Who is experiencing my experience, right now, this very moment?" Don't just think the question—feel it, sense it, in every way you can. Who is present, in yourself, right now? Try to directly intuit it.

The Buddha is reported to have said, "There is no self residing in body and mind, but the cooperation of the conformation produces what people call a person. Paradoxical though it may seem, there is a path to walk on, there is walking to be done, but there is no traveler. There are deeds being done, but no doer. There is blowing of air, but no wind-God behind it that does the blowing. The thought of existing self is an error, and all existences are as hollow as the plantain tree and as empty as twirling water bubbles" (From *The Path of Purification* by Buddhaghosa, translated by Henry Clark Warren, adapted by Jack Kornfield).

This deconstructionist approach to the question "Who am I?" helps us understand that things are not what they seem to be, including our selves. With this insight, we can loosen up and relinquish some of our clinging, our division of things into "mine" and "yours," and our incessant craving: "My house, my car, my mate," "I want," "I need," and "I must have." All of this self-centered and inevitably painful thinking gradually falls apart when we train our minds to see through the illusion that our self is a real and fixed, permanent entity. We begin to evolve into a being more naturally at ease with everyone and everything just as they are, and who wears or enjoys all things, from gross to subtle, visible and invisible, more lightly. To see through ourselves successfully is to untie the knot of heart, loosening one's core organizing principle and opening up a myriad of greater possibilities for freedom and conscious evolution.

Once someone asked me what I had learned in 20 years of Buddhist practice, and I spontaneously said, "I'm not what I think I am." So much of what we think we know, we actually mis-know. We are so identified with who we think we are that it limits how we can be, determines how we live, and conditions how we react. As Mark Twain said, "It's not what we don't know that gets us in trouble, but what we are sure we know." We attach to one or more particular ways of seeing ourselves that, neither accurate nor helpful, entrap us in mind-forged manacles, self-limiting beliefs, and unfulfilling, misdirected behavior patterns and desires. We fall into living as we are not and lose who and what we actually *are*.

Long ago, China's greatest Taoist philosopher Chuang Tsu recounted that one day he dreamt he was a butterfly. When he awoke, he remembered the dream and wondered: "How do I know now that I am a man who dreamt he was a butterfly? How do I know I am not a butterfly dreaming he is a man?"

With the transitory nature of the self in mind, perhaps a better way of phrasing the whole question "Who am I, really and truly?" is "Who am I *being?*" Given that the self is more a process than an entity, the present moment is the one that matters, the one in which we live our life. The past is over, and the future is unknown. We can dwell in the imagined worlds of yesterday and tomorrow if we so choose. But the more we do so, the more we miss out on life itself as it is happening, moment by moment, and the more we fail to realize who we actually are, moment by moment.

Answering the question "Who am I being?" requires monitoring ourselves on a regular basis. If you're a practicing Christian, Jew, or Muslim, for example, one way you can perform this kind of vital, ongoing self-examination is by taking a "God's eye" view of the moment at hand. This means looking at your current self-interests, self-involvements, and conflicts from a more cosmic or divine perspective, the one in which you perceive that God is observing you. The 14th-century Catholic mystic Meister Eckhart alluded to this type of vision when he wrote, "The eye through which I see God is the eye through which God sees me." Thus we know and are known.

The wise Indian guru Nisargadatta Maharaj was once asked, "Is the search for self worth the trouble?" He replied, "Without it all is trouble. If you want to live sanely, creatively, and happily, and have infinite riches to share, search for what you truly are."

Buddhists can be said to conduct the same kind of self-inquiry by choosing the opposite direction—going inward by way of meditation and observing everything that is happening in one's body and mind, heart, and soul. The Dzogchen tradition of Tibetan Buddhism offers rushen meditation to explore the question "Who am I?" Rushen literally means "discerning the difference between." This subtle meditation entails breaking down or challenging our standard, automatic ways of thinking about "self," "body," "mind," personal identity, and other related concepts. Instead of constantly bleating, "What about me?!", we ask ourselves a series of direct but unconventional questions including:

- Who or what is experiencing my present experience? Where is the experiencer? Is it in my head? My brain? My heart? My torso? My consciousness, soul, or spirit?

- What is the essence of my mind? Does the mind have a particular shape? Form? Color? Do I have more than one mind? Is it separate from my body? From other minds?

- Where do my thoughts and feelings come from? Where do they go when they pass on? Is there a source or ground?

- In a moment of non-thought, how is it? What is it? Who and what am I at that moment, free from concepts, beyond mind?

- What is natural and authentic? Unnatural and inauthentic?

- What is happening right now? What is *this*?

My rushen meditation instructions always include "Mind the mind. Turn the spotlight, the searchlight of awareness, *inward*. Look at the one who is looking and feeling; perceive the perceiver; see through the seer and be free." As we engage in answering these kinds of questions during a calm and clear meditative state, without censoring ourselves or worrying about how logical or intelligible our answers may be to others, we can discover all sorts of new information and a richer understanding about who we truly are. We can have a closer encounter with our selves than we've ever had before.

In his book *The Miracle of Mindfulness*, the Zen teacher Thich Nhat Han describes an additional practice we can use to become more aware that our self doesn't end at the boundaries created by our own skin: "Sit in a dark room by yourself, or alone by a river at night, or anywhere else there is solitude. Begin to take hold of your breath. Give rise to the thought, 'I will use my finger to point to myself,' and then, instead of pointing to your body, point away in the opposite direction. Concentrate on seeing yourself outside of your bodily form. Concentrate on seeing your bodily self present before you, in the trees, the grass, the leaves, the river. Be mindful that you are in the universe, and the universe is in you."

I recommend extending this practice beyond meditation into your everyday life, hour by hour as it unfolds. For example, as you look at a person in front of you, whether he or she is someone you like or dislike, say to yourself, "I am interconnected with this person in our shared experience right now as well as on deeper, more subtle, and invisible levels." After all, this person is someone you are experiencing, and someone who is experiencing you, in your shared consensual reality. Moreover, try to extend this empathic connection practice by doing the same with trees you see, dogs you meet or simply hear, foods you taste, and scents you smell. Every moment and everything in the universe further informs you who you are.

This is one way we can practice cultivating, on a daily basis, the radiant moment-to-moment awareness of interbeing, of meaningful connection and profound belonging—of undefended openness and warmhearted oneness with one and all. The less full of ourselves we are, the more room there is for Other—for light to fill us and for divine wisdom and love to enter into this world through us. I had an intuitive insight and wrote long ago in one of my little red travel notebooks:

> *My body is the entire*
> *universe, all beings*
> *my heart and soul.*
> *You are no different.*

4

*God is a circle whose center is everywhere
and circumference nowhere.*

—EMPEDOCLES

Does God Exist?

Is there a supreme, eternal God, and, if so, what kind? What gender, which form? Just which version is actually the right one: Yahweh, The Creator, Lord God, Almighty Father, Allah, Jesus, Brahma, Vishnu, Shiva, any of the other, innumerable names and faces? Where is God? In heaven, above; omnipresent and everywhere; nowhere; transcendent; immanent; totally within? Is God knowable? Or is God the ultimate, inconceivable mystery?

How we conceive of God or the "higher power" is mainly derived from our religious background, upbringing, and culture. No one is free from at least some of this kind of conditioning, and it inevitably provides a lens through which our ideas and beliefs, values and morals, experiences and understanding are all filtered. It thus seems inevitable that there would be different concepts of the highest value or absolute reality and different religions, traditions, and philosophies to express them. I happen to be a Buddhist, but I like to remember Mahatma Gandhi saying that he was a Hindu and Muslim and Christian and Jew, and that to reach the heart of truth was to reach the heart of all religions.

Maybe the answer is in the question. Perhaps the finding of God is inseparable from the longing for God—the seeking, asking, and praying—and the very elusiveness of such an ultimate being. Doesn't that leave room for us to grow into the answer, to continue pursuing it? Now when people ask me, "Does God exist?" I usually reply, "What do you mean by 'God?'" I'm not just being coy. I really need to know before responding to the question, or any talk on the subject is pointless. Are they thinking of God, perhaps, as a personal God, one who cares for us, takes care of us, provides solace, who takes an interest in our individual lives, and to whom we can communicate? The pre-eminent essayist Michel de Montaigne wrote that God is incomprehensible and that everything we think we know about him is a projection of ourselves. And even when the conversation takes place, as valuable as I think it can be, it can't help but remain somewhat beside the point.

I believe that God, in any case, is ultimately beyond clear definition, which accounts for why God has so often been termed nameless, ineffable and inexpressible, formless, the supreme mystery as well as the ultimate good. The philosopher

Michael Henry defines God from a phenomenological point of view. He says, "God is Life, he is the essence of Life, or if we prefer, the essence of Life is God. Saying this, we already know what is God, we know it not by the effect of a learning or of some knowledge, we know not by the thought, on the background of the truth of the world; we know it and we can know it only in and by the Life itself. We can know it only in God."

The seminal medieval thinker and theologian St. Thomas Aquinas said, "God surpasses all things." He said that the first question about God, as about anything else, is the existential question, whether God is, and that "The one thing about God which remains completely unknown in this life is what God is." Finally after a lifetime of study and writing, when he experienced a major mystical epiphany, the saintly philosopher simply said, "It is all like straw," and put away his books and writings.

My Christian minister friends tell me that if you think you want to believe in God, and then you listen to all the arguments presented and remain unconvinced, you have to do something that may seem very strange, but may work out very well in the end. You simply need to realize that faith is a gift from God, ask God for it again and again, and let grace occur in its own time and way.

I am not the faithful true believer who is prone to accepting cultural or familial traditions on faith alone, being more skeptical and inquisitive by nature. In the course of my life, however, I have had a few personal experiences of an intensely spiritual nature that have given me much pause for reflection on the subject of God and the invisible world and have stood me in good stead over the years as touchstones or guiding lights. Each of these experiences gave me a glimpse of God, of oneness and noneness both; and of inconceivable beauty, bliss, belonging, and light. I was absolutely nothing and no one, yet, simultaneously and paradoxically, no less than everything: one with God, one in the creative principle or source of all, one with everything and everyone. I have experienced Heaven on Earth, right here and now, a delicious taste of the Golden Eternity. I have seen that God is totally at home—it is we who are usually out to lunch, wandering astray, daydreaming, sleepwalking, lost in dreams. It was during the most splendid of those mystical experiences that I intuitively understood the saying of St. John: "God is love and whoever abides in love abides in God and God in him." Without theological hairsplitting, godliness doesn't feel much different than Buddhaness—at least in my experience. Spirituality is as spirit does. It is right here; we are usually elsewhere.

Is there one God or many gods, goddesses, and the like? Monotheism sounds like the simpler alternative, but it can actually be very complicated. Many monotheists would say they believe in one supreme God, yet many of them actually believe in a tripartite God: for example, Christians who believe in God as a combination of the Father, Son (Jesus), and Holy Spirit. In this respect, the Christian God is perhaps similar to the supreme god of polytheistic Hinduism, the triune deity of Brahma, Vishnu, and Shiva. I am not a theologian, but when I hear some Buddhists claim with such insouciance and alacrity that God or gods do not exist, I feel it's too easy to say and too hard to know for sure. I want to respond, "Beware of dogmatic assurance. How do you know, after all?" Perhaps it's the inner attorney in me standing up and saying, "Objection, Your Honor—speculative! Unsupported by evidence."

Regarding questions about God's ultimate existence, Buddhism prefers to take a more agnostic—rather than assertively dogmatic—view on the subject, preferring neither *is* nor *is not*, thus remaining true to its renowned Middle Way philosophical principles. For example, Buddha himself did not particularly deny or assert the existence of God; he simply said he didn't need that idea in order to achieve and to teach the path of enlightenment, which was the sole goal of his message. Nor did he advocate proselytizing or spreading Buddhist wisdom; rather, he consistently advocated working on oneself—an inside job that would naturally benefit others through relationships, in ever-widening concentric circles. The problem with so much of organized religion these days is that it too often seems to function as a divisive rather than uniting force, supporting rigid dogmatism, and even fanaticism, rather than the love, inclusiveness, tolerance, and spiritual evolution upon which so many early disciples based their lives. Unfortunately, we can watch such divisiveness playing out in the conflicts and violence that ignited in the name of theology in the Middle East, the Balkans, Ireland, and elsewhere.

I'm Jewish on my parents' side, but Buddhist by choice, training, inclination, and perhaps previous lives, as my Tibetan friends tell me. Throughout Hebrew school, up to my bar mitzvah at age 13, I felt forced to at least hear about, if not reflect upon, questions of God, truth, tradition, belief, cosmology, and history, although not in the most satisfying fashion. My Dad, who was a Jewish believer, once told me after I'd barraged him with questions about God, "Son, be a mensch and God will know you, even if it is impossible to know God." My Dad and my grandmother used to write the unsayable word God with a hyphen, after the Jewish fashion: G-d. For Jewish tradition holds that the Name is too great, too mysterious, too limitless and inconceivable to ever be simply spoken and spelled out, as if a mere object of intellection. As Samuel Butler wrote, "I know not which is the more childish—to deny God, or to define him." When I asked my rabbi in bar mitzvah class about God, he told me God was the Creator and the Father of us all, the source of all goodness and blessings. My follow-up question about who created God led directly to the swift end of our conversation.

When I was in college, I read that Albert Einstein was deeply religious. He said, "Science without religion is lame, religion without science is blind . . . My position concerning God is that of an agnostic. I am convinced that a vivid consciousness of the primary importance of moral principles for the betterment of ennoblement of life does not need the idea of a law-giver, especially a law-giver who works on the basis of reward and punishment." I first felt a genuine interest in God, The Concept, when I read J.D. Salinger's great short

THE BIG QUESTIONS

story "Teddy" in 1968, as a college freshman. "I was six," Teddy says at one point, "when I saw that everything was God, and my hair stood up, and all. It was on a Sunday, I remember. My sister was a tiny child then, and she was drinking her milk, and all of a sudden I saw that she was God and the milk was God. I mean, all she was doing was pouring God into God, if you know what I mean." For some reason, I felt as if I knew what he meant. A few years later I came upon a very similar thought, in the Bhagavad Gita, the "Song of God," the sacred Hindu scripture. In the Katha Upanishad, one of India's ancient scriptures, I read: "He is one, the lord and innermost Self of all; of one form, he makes of himself many forms."

In early 1973, while visiting my family in the U.S. after my first years in India, I attended sesshins (intensive weeklong meditation retreats) with Sazaki Roshi, one of the most elderly Japanese Zen masters in the West, still alive and in his 90s today. Until that time I had rarely heard a Buddhist master utilize the word "God" in his teachings, when suddenly during a private interview, he presented me with the Zen koan (meditation conundrum): "How to realize God while driving car?" For a few years I saw Sazaki on and off, and he'd drive me crazy with that koan, until I came up with a genuine answer expressing some modicum of authentic realization.

As a young seeker, I wrote this prayerful reflection in one of the little red pocket notebooks I used to carry on the Overland Route across the Middle East and on into India:

I am with God and in God forever;
I have no existence apart from that.
Who cares if anyone loves me, or even if everyone does?
Love is found through loving; God loves me,
and I am love.
God, guru and oneSelf are one.

Today I might replace the word God with the word Buddha in the poem, to make my Buddhist constituents happy; but how many among us can really say the two terms—neither of which are easily or completely understood—are not almost synonymous? Perhaps these words, rather than reliable technical terms, are more like placeholders for concepts beyond the reach of our current language.

Between 1972 and 1974, I lived for several months in the Gandhi ashrams of northern India. There I read Mahatma Gandhi's books, encountered a few of his last living disciples, learned about milking goats as well as about prayer, yoga, meditation, vegetarianism, non-violence (ahimsa), and the power of truth (satyagraha). Like so many, I too was deeply inspired by the Great Soul (Mahatma), whose incandescent spirit and non-violent, wisdom-based leadership ignited India's liberation from Colonial rule. He wrote, "There are innumerable definitions of God, because his manifestations are innumerable. But I worship God as truth only. The absolute truth, the eternal principle, that is God. To me, God is love. God is sat-chit-ananda, as the scriptures say: truth-knowledge-bliss. God is ethics and morality;

God is fearlessness. God is the source of light and life, and yet he is above and beyond all these things. God is omniscient, omnipresent, mysterious, all-powerful and merciful. He is all things to all men."

The peerless international Buddhist scholar and Zen master, D.T. Suzuki, author of 95 books about Zen and enlightenment, while a graduate student in Germany had done his PhD thesis on Meister Eckhart's mystical understanding of God as pure Being itself (no thing), rather than as a discreet being (thing). "What?!?" I thought, "God as nothingness? Not supreme being, not creator, not eternal Big Kahuna, not all-knowing divine intelligence, omnipotent master of the universe—but God as similar if not identical to Mahayana Buddhism's concept of *sunyata*: voidness, emptiness, the absolute ground of being (as opposed to the relative nature of things)?" What a shock this was to the youthful Buddhist I was at the time!

To echo Eckhart, God is not a thing, but is hidden, a being beyond even being. Eckhart thought that God is not found in the soul by adding anything, but instead by the process of subtraction, elimination—as in his famous "via negativa", the way of nothingness—a more fundamental notion than even discrete Being itself. Meister Eckhart famously prayed to God to be rid of God, saying, "The highest, most lofty thing that one can let go of is to let go of God for the sake of God." Eckhart thought the most beautiful thing a person could say about God would be to remain silent from a wisdom of inner wealth. "If the only prayer you ever say in your entire life is 'Thank you,' that would be enough."

Many Buddhists in Asia commonly pray to Buddha or to their guru, just as Westerners pray to their One God and Hindus to their gods and gurus. In the ultimate analysis, if pressed, I would say that it probably doesn't matter much who or what you pray to, or how, why, and what for. I simply trust that the Central Switchboard sorts out and translates all the different prayers and wishes and needs accordingly. My brother, a rational scientist and superb mathematician, claims to be an agnostic, although since he was gifted with a daughter in his mid-forties, he is consistently marveling at how there must be a beneficent God in order to account for such a miracle as her new life. It looks to me like a mighty struggle between head and heart; his conscious mind can't accept religion and notions such as a universal creator God, while his instincts seem to be telling him otherwise. The Venerable Thich Nhat Han says, "Praying is asking for help, and in the Buddhist tradition we ask the Buddha to help us. If our friends in Christianity see that God is the Spirit—the collective mind from which everything manifests—then the distance separating Buddhism and Christianity would not be much at all."

I think the word God is a fine placeholder to symbolize the highest, the ultimate, the supreme, the eternal and transcendent, however we may conceive of, imagine, or idealize it. I often enjoy the way in which some people today employ the phrase "higher power" to sum up their belief in something transcending this transitory, mundane world. The phrase leaves room for others' beliefs in a similarly vague, mysterious, yet deeply felt higher power—by whatever name form or formless notion—thus infusing a more infinite, timeless, deeper meaning and purpose to people's short and somewhat troubled lives. When I think of God, I am no longer thinking of nor reacting against the child's image of the white bearded, awesome elderly gentleman sitting above us in judgment in the clouds. When I notice crosses, six-pointed stars, church steeples, cathedral towers, Buddhist stupa and temple spires, the expansive domes and up-reaching minarets of mosques, I see pointers leading beyond—all but touching something that is beyond, a common higher ground including us all yet beyond each of us—totally transcendent, yet mysteriously immanent in all of us and each of us. We should not mistake the pointers, the religious symbols, but let them direct our inner gaze further, deeper, truer to the ultimate reality, however we or our elders or/and their traditions may conceive, express, or imagine it.

The Buddha rarely if ever discussed God—theism is not a central part of Buddha's path to awakened enlightenment, peace, and deathless nirvana. Whether there is a God or not is one of the 14 questions that Buddha famously refused to speculate about or entertain, mainly because he was intent upon people seeking and finding the deepest truth about reality through their own experience. Several of his disciples even tried to engage him in theological discussions—to which he consistently replied that he would neither deny nor affirm the existence of deities or a supreme deity because such speculative talk was futile and a distraction, not conducive to the path of awakening he taught. Buddhism as a religion does not resonate with or embrace most people's idea of God or gods, mainly because the wisdom of enlightenment revealed to Buddha that there is no separate, supreme being or eternal creator deity, nor immortal gods, outside the laws of karma (cause and effect), interconnectedness, and impermanence. Need I ask, as Buddhist logicians do: If God is the first principle—the first cause—then who created the creator? Who or what moved the first movement into movement?

Buddha actually accepted and took for granted the existence of higher beings like Shiva, Vishnu, Brahma, and the other devas (long-lived gods, demigods, archangels) of which he was aware: remember Buddha lived 500 years before the time of Jesus, 1,100 years before Mohammed and the rise of Islam. For him, these *devas* would have naturally played a part in life and the life of people he talked to, and he didn't deny their existence. He did deny that making ritual offerings and sacrifices to please them would bring what people needed and were ultimately seeking. This is not to deny the positive aspects of faith, devotion, awe—recognizing something greater than ourselves, whatever it may be—and the beauty of prayer and the efficacy of being able to ask for help, including the humble willingness to surrender and give thanks and so forth.

When Westerners would ask the late Venerable Kalu Rinpoche, my first root guru, if he believed in God, he'd reply, "Which God?" There are many different ways people believe in God. I feel that perhaps knowledge and experience of God develops in the pursuit of the question rather than residing somewhere as the answer to it. Perhaps it's more productive, let alone accurate, to think of God as a verb rather than a noun, as an energy rather than an entity. Rainer Maria Rilke, one of my favorite poets, suggested that we think of God as a direction rather than as an object. That direction is towards the best and highest that we can conceive.

Can something exist if we can't precisely define it? Of course it can! We generally regard the term "God" as representing a power, being, or frame of reference that is higher than the human one. Theologian Paul Tillich said that God is *being* itself, not a being. That very understanding implies that human beings are unable to define or imagine God with precise clarity. When it comes to determining whether something as indefinable as God exists, we simply have to rely on other ways of addressing the question than through logic or linear, sequential thought. Father John Bridleigh, an Anglican priest, writes, "You can't define God with any words, just as you can't confine God under the dome of any temple. As a true believer, you're left with the expression, 'God is.'" My friend Rabbi David Cooper feels much the same way. He once told me, "God is not a thing, a being, a noun." Instead, David prefers to think of God as an endlessly radiating and interactive expression. Although he practices Buddhist meditation as well as Jewish rituals, he certainly seems to believe in God, at least in a Kabbalistic way.

Many intelligent people who profess to believe in God's existence accept the fact that God remains a mystery and always will, and that mysterious and unknowability are intrinsic characteristics of God. In fact, they characterize God as the never-to-be-explained force or presence that's at the heart of things, giving the animate and inanimate their own miraculous existence. Among the thinkers who fit into this category are some of my greatest personal heroes. Albert Einstein, for instance, claimed, "To know that what is impenetrable to us really exists, manifesting itself as the highest wisdom and the most radiant beauty . . . this knowledge, this feeling is at the center of true religiousness. In this sense, and in this sense only, I belong to the rank of devoutly religious men." Mahatma Gandhi once remarked, "I claim to be a passionate seeker after truth, which is but another name for God." For me, it's difficult if not impossible to insist that God *doesn't* exist when such admirable, sane, even wise, yet practical, individuals firmly believe the opposite.

Gandhi's statement in particular guides us toward yet another manner of thinking about God—that is, considering God as the ultimate reality or the absolute way. In the Jewish and Christian traditions, we see this concept of God reflected in his Biblical role as the fundamental lawgiver. The Book of Genesis opens with the phrase, "In the beginning was the Word," which many theologians have interpreted to mean that God is, in essence, the prime intelligence, or, more colloquially, the "final word." This perspective is remarkably similar to the Eastern religious concepts of Tao and Dharma, each of which can be roughly defined as "the true way" or "the ultimate law of the universe." Not far from the meaning of the original Biblical term *logos*, usually translated as the "word" in modern Bibles.

Because the Buddha was not a God, Buddhism is not a theistic religion—one based on the worship of a God. But that doesn't mean it's an atheistic religion—one that doesn't believe that God exists. It's more accurate to call it non-theistic. It doesn't take up the question of whether or not there's an omnipotent creator God, like the Jewish, Christian, or Muslim God. This is not mere wordplay, but represents the kind of fine distinctions that any nuanced discussion about such a profound subject necessarily entails.

I personally associate God with the inherent splendor and coherence of the universe, not far from what people loosely think of as a state of grace, or Oneness. Although as a Buddhist teacher I don't commonly use the word God in this way, you could say I believe God exists as infinite wholeness and perfection. I believe we experience God whenever we have intimations of this all-inclusive completeness and overarching continuity in our lives, whenever we think, speak, or act in a manner that reinforces our interrelationship with everything else. The less our egocentric self gets in the way, the more room there is for God, or any meaningful conception, or for Buddha, and for love itself.

Instead of asking ourselves, "Does God exist?," I think a better way of putting the question is "What is the most fundamental, primordial, underlying substratum of our existence right here and now—the very bedrock of reality? "We need to inquire into that matter so deeply, honestly, and persistently that we contact and connect with that. For if it is everywhere and eternal (as most people believe God is), it must also be here and now. Rabbi David Aaron has said, "God is not a being, existing in reality. God 'is' reality. We exist in this reality. We exist within God. To find God, you have to ask yourself, 'Where am I?' not, 'Where is God?' God isn't in any particular place. God is the place and everyplace. We live in God."

I like the story about Ralph Waldo Emerson, our first American philosopher—I feel akin to the old Concord transcendentalist—who said after his most singularly earth-shaking spiritual epiphany, "I am a transparent eye-ball." This view is reminiscent of the great mystic Meister Eckhart's statement, "The eye with which I see God is the eye with which he sees me. My eye and the eye of God are one eye, one vision, one knowledge and one love."

Children by nature possess a much livelier intelligence and imagination than most adults, and they have repeatedly given me keen insights into the existence of God. Once, after a retreat, I was invited to a Montessori school in Austin, Texas, to talk with a class of 9-year-olds. The kids came bursting into the room and climbed all over me, as I was sitting down on the floor in their circle—it was a great, playful beginning! In the same spirit, I ended our time together with a special gong meditation that you might try sometime. Before I hit the gong, I asked the kids to watch the sound, see where it went, and follow it. I told them it might bring them closer to the Buddha, to God. I used both terms—the Buddha and God—for several reasons: I was talking with them as a Buddhist; they were more familiar with the idea of God; and I genuinely believe that focusing on either the Buddha or God can take us to the same "place," which is nowhere and everywhere, now here.

A week later, the mother of one of the kids reported to me what he told her about the activity. "I watched the sound of the gong disappear, and I followed it," he said. "I went there, and you know what, Mom? When I went there, I didn't feel I was *closer* to God or the Buddha—I *was* God."

5

The world is too dangerous for anything but truth and too small for anything but love.

—WILLIAM SLOANE COFFIN

What Is Love and How Do I Find It?

There is possibly only one question that seekers need to ask themselves about their spiritual progress (and, assuming they believe in Heaven, the only one they'll be tested on should they wish entrance through the Pearly Gates at death): "How well have I loved?" Learning how to love is the goal and the purpose of a spiritual life. Love is the way, the truth, and the light that is common to all religions and humanistic philosophies. How can a good person live a good life today, in our troubled world? Mother Teresa said, "It is not how much we do, but how much love we put into the doing. It is not how much we give, but how much love we put into the giving."

Valentine's Day is one of my favorite American holidays. The fact that this heart-centered (if over-commercialized) day falls annually around the same time as Tibetan New Year reminds me to make New Year's resolutions regarding those I love and to renew my commitment to cultivate goodness of heart and warm caring in all my relationships. These resolutions usually involve opening my heart and mind, listening more attentively, learning to forgive and love even those I don't like or agree with, and coming to accept and bless the world, rather than fighting with it or trying to escape from it. As the seminal Zen Master Dogen says, "To practice the Buddha Way is to be intimate with all things."

Some say we are here in this world to learn and to evolve in consciousness. Primary among life's lessons is how to love and to love well, and how to *be* love—to live it and be loving, embodied as compassion, empathy, and selfless caring in action—as well as to receive love. I believe love is central to happiness, satisfaction, growth, meaning, and fulfillment. In his book *Teachings on Love,* Thich Nhat Han writes, "Happiness is only possible with true love. True love has the power to heal and transform the situation around us and bring a deep meaning to our lives. There are people who understand the nature of true love and how to generate and nurture it. The teachings on love given by the Buddha are clear, scientific and applicable. Every one of us can benefit from these teachings."

How would Jesus love? *Agapé,* or caritas—Christian love—is self-giving, unconditional love. It is the very heart of the Good Samaritan, the guardian angels, and the Bodhisattva, the selfless Buddhist superhero. In the Bible it is written, "Greater love has no man than this, that a man lay down his life for his friends." How, then, would Buddha love? By seeing every single being, human and otherwise, as fundamentally like and equal to himself, thus enabling him to naturally treat and love others in the way he himself would choose to be treated. We call this infinitely benevolent, selfless love *Bodhichitta,* or the Awakened Heart—the very spirit of enlightenment. Buddha taught, "Putting down all barriers, let your mind be full of love. Let it pervade all the quarters of the world so that the whole wide world, above, below, and around, is pervaded with love. Let it be sublime and beyond measure so that it abounds everywhere." The Buddhist practices of metta (lovingkindness) and Bodhichitta (selfless altruism as love in action) teach us how to cultivate and develop this noble hearted love and impartial compassion in daily life.

Unconditional love is inseparable from authenticity and inner freedom. It is a law unto itself, a love that is totally proactive and appropriately responsive, not merely blindly reactive. Love creates its own wake, has its own direction, moves according to its own rhythm, and makes its own music. True love has no sides, boundaries, or corners. It is without circumference and beyond inside and out. The heart of limitless love includes everyone and everything, embracing one and all in its warmth.

Genuine love is enough in simply being itself. Love finds its own way and creates its own universe. Love-practice combines selflessness, generosity, empathy, meaningful connection, cherishment, and oneness. Love is indubitably found through loving. Buddha taught, "Putting aside all barriers, let your mind be full of love. Let it pervade all the quarters of the world so that the whole wide world, above, below, and around, is pervaded with love."

"We need love, we need beauty, and we need at least passing acquaintance with eternity. To the soul these are absolutes, and yet in modern life these three graces of life are values largely neglected. We reduce love to interpersonal relationship and then treat relationship as an emotional problem . . . The soul longs for love that is unconditional, unending and without tangible object," writes Thomas Moore, contemporary writer and philosopher.

There are so many kinds of love and subtleties of love. The word love, like truth and God, is hard to define with precision. Today we associate love mainly with romantic feelings, but this is a limited view. Although we can talk about brotherly love, parental love, filial love, love of work, and love of beauty, justice, nature, God, and so forth, there are basically three separate categories of love with which we are all habitually involved:

1. *Instinctive love*: This is the love that many people call chemistry. Instinctive love happens when we are drawn toward another human being by a combination of karma, powerful pheromones, and subtle energy. Love at this level can be like a magic spell, which everyone knows may deceive us and produce all kinds of unwanted results. We sometimes call it romance, physical desire, lust, or passion; I prefer the term instinctive love. Instinctive love can provide the basis for a deeper, more emotional love, as it develops into mature and longer-lasting bonds.

2. *Emotional love*: This love makes us feel connected and bonded. We feel this kind of love for our parents, siblings, mates, children, kindred spirits, and friends. With some people we feel so connected that we use the expression soul mates. Emotional love often starts with a sense of liking someone and finding things in common; from that, love builds and grows deeper over time as we learn to trust and open our hearts.

3. *Conscious love*: We often refer to conscious love as unconditional love or divine love. Of all types of love, this is the hardest to cultivate. Conscious love describes the ability to love without reservations or agendas. I use the term conscious because this love rests on a firm foundation of intentionality. It's no accident; it doesn't evolve from lust, fantasy, or needs; we don't expect anything in return, beyond the radiant joy of simply loving. This is sacred love, selfless love—unconditional, boundless, and groundless.

If we look carefully, I think we would discover that we are immersed in love. The moment we are born, we begin learning about love and loving from those who care for us, before understanding either words or concepts. The ability to love well and wisely is the most important trait that parents can pass on to their children. How to share it and how to receive it can and must develop from that base as we grow throughout our lives. Parents, grandparents, and other beloveds love us even after they are dead and gone: Their love remains actively present in our psyches, our inner world. Close friends love us. Many feel that God loves us. Love in all its forms is heartwarming and heart-opening. Divine Buddha-like love surrounds and enfolds us when we are open to it. Love's multi-dimensional lessons are here to be learned, for those who love.

The archetypal image of Buddhist love is the four-armed Avalokitesvara, known as Chenrayzig in Tibet and Kuan Yin in China. Buddha taught that this Bodhichitta, or spiritual love, has four active arms, each representing one of the Four Boundless Attitudes: lovingkindness, compassion, sympathetic joy, and equanimity.

- The first arm of Buddhist love is maitri, or lovingkindness, a boundless feeling of friendliness and well-wishing toward others. Maitri, or *metta* in the Pali language, implies friendliness: befriending and accepting yourself along with others, including your body and mind, feelings, energy and emotions, and the entire world.

- The second is karuna, or compassion, based on heartfelt empathy—being moved by feeling what others feel, thus being impelled to help.

- The third arm is mudita: spiritual joy and satisfaction. This includes rejoicing in the virtue and success of others—the antidote to envy and jealousy.

- The fourth arm is upeksha: equanimity. This is the ability to recognize equality in all that lives. This impartial recognition leads to the wisdom of objectivity and detachment, rather than indifference or complacence, which are its near enemies. We cannot love like Jesus or Buddha if we love some while ignoring or even mistreating others.

Buddhist love is based on recognizing our fundamental interconnectedness. It knows that all beings are like ourselves in wanting and needing happiness, safety, fulfillment, and belonging, and not wanting suffering and misery. The Dalai Lama has said, "If you want to be wisely selfish, care for others." We need each other to become enlightened, because the development of genuine wisdom depends on developing warmhearted love and compassion. All the happiness and virtue in this world come from selflessness and generosity, all the sorrow from egotism, selfishness, and greed. Buddha's constant companion, the monk Ananda, once approached him and said: "Enlightened Master, is it true, as I have heard, that spiritual friendship is fully half of the holy life?" Buddha, a monk who might be thought of as a solitary individual and meditator, simply replied, "No, Ananda, that is not so. Spiritual friendship is the *whole* of the holy life." Each relationship and every single encounter can be a vehicle for love-practice, coupled with meaningful spiritual connection, through the transformative magic of warmhearted Bodhichitta. This is how we love, Buddha-style: unselfishly impartial to all, free from excessive attachment or false hope and expectation, accepting, tolerant, and forgiving.

Seminal Jewish thinker Martin Buber taught that life is all about encounter and relationship—how we meet one another. The holy spirit's temple is not a body, but a relationship. When you meet anyone, consider it a holy encounter. Consider that person as a mirror—in that person, you'll find yourself or lose yourself. Recently when I talked with therapists at an annual Psychotherapy and Meditation conference in Cambridge, they all said that most people's problems center on their relationships. From the teen years until quite late in life, the majority of people talk most of the time about their relationships or lack of relationships. "What about me?" is a common complaint.

This all points to the necessity for opening up our relationships to spiritual inquiry and more meaningful forms of growth. In order to walk a living path today, to live the vital flame of Dharma, I think we need to practice the art of wise relationships, mindful of connecting and disconnecting. We need to learn how to cultivate relationships that are balanced, appropriate, directed towards oneness and reconciliation, as well as tolerant of differences. We need to open up our relationships for spiritual practice; for bringing mindfulness and attention to bear; for seeing clearly what's going on; for opening our hearts, for cultivating more generosity, lovingkindness, and empathy; and for seeing the light, the Buddha, or God—whatever you call it—in others. We know we can see the light in our child or our pet dog or cat, but what about in our colleagues or the people that scare us on the street, or the kinds of insects we're afraid of? Can we perceive the light, the divine, Buddha-nature, in all?

Human love can open us to divine love, the boundlessness of unconditional loving. We have to begin somewhere. Intimate personal relationships can be enhanced and sublimated into Relationship Yoga through cultivating relational mindfulness, making sacred our interactions as a way toward union and oneness with something greater than any of us, yet accessible in and through each of us. Through human consciousness we can touch cosmic consciousness, which we might occasionally also experience through the ecstatic consummation of physical passion, or in the unconditional love we feel, for example, for our newborn child. Through opening our self-protective cocoon and letting others in, which is part of intimate loving with or without physical contact, we can momentarily lose our egocentric selves and touch a deep and more universal dimension, where all meet and are joined.

We can think globally about universal love and compassion, but we have to start somewhere. Let's think globally but act locally—with ourselves and with each other. Warm human affection, as His Holiness the Dalai Lama said, is the most important thing in life. If we let love touch us deeply, it softens us up and warms our hearts. Human love is the tip of the iceberg of divine love, one small part of a bigger love. This is a spiritual practice—not only truth, but loving.

Wisdom and compassion together are the two wings of the spirit soaring in the space of awakening. Without this balance, we become only creatures of the head, or, on the other hand, maybe just creatures of the heart, blown about by our emotional energies, feelings, and unbalanced thoughts. Rabbi Abraham Joshua Heschel writes, "Love and Truth are the two ways that lead the soul out of the inner jungle. Love offers an answer to the question of how to live. In Truth we find an answer to the question of how to think. It is impossible to find Truth without warmhearted love, and it is impossible to experience love without being truthful, without living Truth."

When we consider loving as holy encounter, as sacred relationship-making, we notice various dimensions of relating to one another through such interbeing. These dimensions can be characterized as a deepening, and not entirely linear, process:

1. Approaching

2. Making contact, connecting

3. Entering, or feeling more connected

4. Engaging and experiencing feeling

5. Going even deeper, while sustaining and attuning

6. Communicating, communing, exchanging, flowing even deeper

7. Commingling and joining (previous stages necessary before reaching this stage)

8. Merging and dissolving, being more present and disappearing at the same time

9. Uniting, becoming wholeness; entering into the mysterious union of oneness and noneness

Perhaps by reflecting on both the previous list of different kinds of love and this experiential depth chart of the spectrum of intimate contacts and dimensions of love, we may become more mindful of them in our daily lives. These thoughts will enable us to become more truly intimate with everyone and everything in the universe. We will harbor fewer unrealistic demands and expectations, and enjoy more cling-free, joyously spontaneous relationships.

In Indian yoga, which offers an entire, well-rounded system of spiritual life (well beyond simple physical movements), human relationships are explicitly understood as arenas for spiritual practice. The word yoga actually means union or reunion. It has a similar derivation etymologically as the word religion, which means to unite or rejoin. The system includes the yogas of meditation, energy and heat practices, bhakti (or devotion), and karma (or service to God and humanity). Hindu lay people understand their homes to be temples and marriage a holy sacrament. Marriage vows are held to be equally sacred as monastic vows or vows of renunciation. Serving God through serving one's mate and by extension, one's family, and by extension, one's community, and by extension, one's entire community of all beings, is one of the main ways to reach God or union or spiritual realization, according to one of the most ancient and populous traditions of the world. Hinduism teaches us to venerate our mate as Shiva or Shakti, God or Goddess. This is very different from the puritanical notion that being married is some kind of worldly distraction or hindrance.

From the point of view of spiritual life, the purpose of relationship is to help us each awaken our hearts—our own best, loving selves. I myself have had many gurus, Eastern masters of all different schools and traditions. Besides all of these mostly male figures, some of my best teachers were the lovers and women in my life. They were like gurus, reflecting who I am and what I could be, including limitations, foibles, hang-ups, strengths, and talents. They were great yoga instructors. They were great awareness teachers. They were great trainers of the mind and refiners of the heart. In their best aspects, they were masters of the heart's love and body's passion for loving union. Intimate relationships have provoked many of my growth moments.

Love leads us beyond ourselves, and helps us be who we really *are*. So we should ask ourselves what we are seeking in others. What are we really looking for? What needs and expectations do we expect others to fulfill? What is driving our relationships? Are we dispassionately committed to our lover's best and highest interest, or to her only so long as she is making us feel good, assuaging our loneliness, and chasing away fear and boredom? Antoine De Saint-Exupéry wrote,

"Love does not consist of gazing at each other, but in looking together in the same direction." See God in the mate, and you get to God. See Buddha in the Guru, you get to Buddha. Such sacred vision comes from bringing ourselves, whole and complete, to our relationships. This sacred way of seeing is actually a daily-life practice we can cultivate, called Pure Perception.

People seem to be afraid of the deeper implications of being themselves in wholeness and completeness—independence and autonomy—misunderstanding what it can actually signify. Some have said to me, "If I am complete as I am, why do I need anyone else?" They pose this as a problem, not understanding that if they are not whole and complete—that is, free from grasping and craving—no one else can really complete and satisfy them. Being whole and complete is not about fierce, independent isolationism, but rather realizing one's place in the whole, while also realizing the entirety as in each particular part.

It is in our heart and soul's higher self-interest to strive to become more integrated and complete within ourselves. By doing so, we can enter more deeply into sacred loving and the promise of oneness through intimate relations. One-half plus one-half does not equal one; one whole plus one whole equals relational *oneness*. The essence of Buddhist relationship is to cultivate the cling-free relationship. When we find our own wholeness, we can enter our relationships more fully, as complete beings with hearts open to love and passion, enriched with caring and equanimity. As St. Paul wrote in his *Letter to the Corinthians*: "If I speak with the languages of men and of angels, but don't have love, I have become sounding brass, or a clanging cymbal . . . Love is patient, love is kind. It does not envy, it does not boast, it is not proud. It is not rude, it is not self-seeking, it is not easily angered, it keeps no record of wrongs. Love does not delight in evil, but rejoices in the truth. It always protects, it always trusts, it always hopes, it always perseveres. Love never fails . . . Faith, hope and love remain— these three—but the greatest of these is love."

We all feel the desire to love and be loved, to hold and be held, to connect, belong, and be embraced. However, I think that the most important thing in being together is the tenderness of a warm heart, a connected feeling. If our relationships aren't nurturing the growth and development of goodness of heart, openness, generosity, authenticity, and intimate connection, they are not serving us or furthering a better world.

Sometimes love requires letting go, as well as stick-to-itiveness, perseverance, and patient forbearance. Sooner or later, growing children have to go their own ways before our mothering becomes smothering; loved ones often move on in one way or another. Through these experiences we must eventually learn to loosen our grip, allow, accept, and let be. Change and loss are significant parts of any life and cannot be avoided, yet they can be met gracefully, genuinely, heartfully. Sometimes the most loving choice can be to let someone go and let be, painful, awkward, and stressful as it may initially seem. Sadness and grief can also be expressions of love and need not be suppressed. Proceeding through the stages of healthy and conscious grieving is far better than taking an emotional bypass down the river of denial or through the endlessly winding caverns of suppression, repression, and avoidance. In truly loving others, I have learned that I need to let them be and to accept and appreciate them as they are (free of my projections and illusions), not as I would like them to be. This is equally true for loving and accepting oneself.

In India in the 1970s, I used to cultivate love for my late father, with whom I had significant conflict during my youth, by practicing with the recollection-phrase, "He loves me so much that he. . . ." Each time I completed the statement with some way he expressed his love for me, often by doing something in order to satisfy or help me, or giving up something small or large, momentary or monumental. I would recite this over and over again as a spiritual love and gratitude-deepening practice. This gratitude-oriented reflection greatly helped heal my relationship with my dad, both in my inner psyche and later in our personal interactions during time together. Spiritual practice is such an incredible way to use our human capacities, including love, passionate intimacy, and longing for connection and pleasure, to take us beyond egotism and selfishness, bitterness, resentment and confusion. It's so useful because it helps us to really be our best selves, inhabit the high ground, and love people even when we may not always like what they do.

Don't we still manage to love our children, even though sometimes we don't always like what they do? Can all of our relationships go in that direction? Can we cultivate a love that's even bigger than only loving our children or mates or parents? Can we let it grow, so that we love many others, everyone, including all the animals and creatures—even the ones we don't like? Can we love the criminal and the sinner even while we abhor the crime, the sin? Can we learn to be helpful or empathic even to people who are violent or aggressive? Can we realize that we are all "children of God," even if some of us are truly naughty ones? Can we dislike the action while still loving the child?

Unconditional love can manifest itself in many surprising ways: light, dark, sweet, soft, firm, and even fierce. For instance, in the story of Jesus driving the money changers from the temple, we find his expression of deepest, unconditional love came through intense, firm action based on clear knowing. It is beneficial in thinking about expressions and practices of love to realize that they don't necessarily all involve a romantically "nice" surface appearance, depending on the underlying intentions and motivations involved in that love.

The Beatles sang, "All you need is love." The ancient Roman poet Virgil said, "Love conquers all." We all want to believe that and many of us do—but is it true? Perhaps in the highest ultimate spiritual and divine sense, yes, for sure. But for most of us, most of the time, down here on Earth where we live and breathe, eat, and excrete, I am sorry to say that I have found that love is not enough. What about truth? Authenticity? Health, peace, harmony? This is where the other noble virtues come into play. They are in all of us, but they need to be realized, cultivated, and developed. Without them, how can we actively engage in intimate relationships? This is why there are ten virtues in the Buddhist practice of loving:

1. Unselfishness and selflessness (while also taking care of yourself)

2. Generosity, giving of yourself

3. Patience, forbearance, tolerance, acceptance

4. Respect, honor, trust, support

5. Honesty, communication, revealing yourself, truth-telling

6. Empathy, compassion, caring

7. Delight, joy, pleasure, play (Don't take all of this or yourself so seriously!)

8. Wonderment, paying attention, taking interest, listening, appreciation

9. Being open to mystery, to not knowing, to not having it all worked out

10. Sensing a shared mission, purpose, direction, ideal or goal

We all want and need love. Love is the center of human life. In fact, most of us almost constantly seek it—often more than anything else in life. That's because like seeks like, and we *are* love. We all have hearts of love. We are the energy of love, like the invisible God's visible body of love, or Buddha's body of love manifesting in this world. It happens through us. Love is not just something we do or experience. Buddha showed us a way of transforming ourselves so that we are able to *be* love, purely and unconditionally. Love is our most beautiful and unobscured way of being. It is our truest and deepest calling, summoning forth the divine being, the Buddhaness, within each and all of us.

Seeing oneself in others and others in oneself is the key to accomplishing oneness through Relationship Yoga. This relational mindfulness helps us to practice the Golden Rule and treat others as we ourselves would be treated. Learning to consciously slow down and pay attention enough to feel what others feel—utilizing the nine steps to intimacy or the ten virtues outlined above, for example—allows us to empathize and sympathize with another, which is the root of compassion, altruism, and selflessness. In this way we can genuinely love our way to enlightenment.

6

All that we are is the result of what we have thought. If a man speaks or acts with an evil thought, pain follows him. If a man speaks or acts with a pure thought, happiness follows him, like a shadow that never leaves him.

—BUDDHA, *THE DHAMMAPADA* (THE SAYINGS)

What Is Karma, and How Can I Manage It in My Life?

American Express recently received the Best Spot Award from *Ad Week* magazine for their tagline, "American Express: The official card of good karma." The accompanying advertisement shows the L.A. Lakers' highly successful coach, Phil Jackson, stopping by a convenience store and purchasing a lottery card and bottle of soda with a prize-winning cap. Will he win the lottery, too? And what, if anything, does *this* have to do with karma?

Today the Sanskrit word karma shows up on TV sitcoms, in movies, at school, in the office, and even on the sports page of the newspaper. People often mistake it to mean variously luck, fate or destiny, determinism, predestination, fatalism, or blame, although karma literally means just action-reaction. Karma is understood in Eastern thought as the law of cause and effect: What goes around, comes around; as we sow, we shall reap. Karma means conditioning, to put it psychologically. All our chickens eventually come home to roost, as my Midwestern friends used to say.

Actually, the law of karma is slightly more developed and subtly nuanced than the important but quite general "reaping what we have sown" Sunday school lesson. The law of karmic causation reveals to us that nothing happens by accident, and that everything has a cause or causes, however subtle or invisible they may be. Everything is part of large, subtle patterns; for every action there's a reaction, as the scientific laws of motion have discovered. This places the steering wheel of our own lives squarely in our hands and reminds us that the better we understand life's universal underlying principles—those regarding impermanence, mortality, contingency and interconnectedness, ethical values, and causation—the better off we are.

Karma need not be a foreign, mystical, airy fairy concept; it means that everything counts. Everything we do and think and say matters, on some level at least. My self-patented Dharma for Dummies (Like Me) approach distills the essence of reams of karma theory into this one essential lesson: No one other than oneself creates or is ultimately responsible for one's own happiness and suffering, which we more or less create by ourselves for ourselves. Everything is so subjective; it is not what happens to us but what we make of it that makes all the difference. Of course that is not to say we are all free from outside influences.

It is not simply that our mind creates everything. And yet, no one high or low, outside or inside, visible or invisible, human or otherwise, has ultimate power over us, as far as our inherent character, life experience, and perceived karmic destiny are concerned. For "character is destiny," as Heraclitus famously said. The three most common errors we make regarding the ancient, timeless, cosmic, and eminently practical teachings of karma are:

- Assuming that our karma is somehow fated or predestined; believing fatalistically that we have a fixed future and that our karma is scripted or written in concrete

- Feeling helpless in the face of karma

- Mistaking the sovereign source of agency as totally above and beyond ourselves, when we are in fact responsible for ourselves and our own actions and states of mind, and, thus, our personal karma

Karma, meaning causation, details the inexorable laws of cause and effect. It reveals all things as interdependent; every action has a reaction, and nothing exists in absolute isolation.

The law of karma expands to explain the primary and secondary cause of things, the mechanics of interdependent origination and interconnectedness, and how to be free of karmic reactivity, unwholesome patterns and thought processes, and unskillful, unhelpful conditioning. Thus we come to understand that our experiences and states of mind and heart are the results of previous seeds we have sown, that these karmic seeds or imprints can be mitigated or even destroyed before coming to fruition, and that we do not necessarily have to suffer the full results of our karma if our inner wisdom is fully and correctly functioning.

Karma is not fatalism, as if things are predetermined, scripted, inevitably fixed, and totally beyond our active agency/control, as some people might mistakenly think. Karma depends fundamentally on motivation and intention. Gautama Buddha himself said, "Wherever we go, wherever we remain, the results of our actions follow us. As we think so we become." Our karma is the one thing we carry with us always, even beyond the grave—or so 'tis said.

In the karmic view so central to Eastern thought, there are no accidents. Everything has causes. To realize how karma works through insight into its actual mechanics is to become master rather than victim of our fate, and to realize freedom from and even autonomy within causes, circumstances, and conditions. That is why Buddha said, "No one can make me angry unless I have the seeds of anger inside." These seeds are the main cause, and external events are the contributing causes that help ripen the seeds within. Thus, ultimately, no one can make us happy or sad, although they—their thoughts and actions, words and will—may very well supply a contributing or supportive cause. Since the pursuit of happiness and freedom seems so vitally important to most of us, it would be beneficial if we could penetrate more deeply into the mysteries regarding where and how these illusory karmic ideals can be discovered and ultimately attained.

The doctrine of karma fundamentally teaches and reveals to us that feelings—positive and negative—flow from within in a pattern of widening ripples as the outcome of pleasant or unpleasant experiences resulting from other past actions, intentions, thoughts, and feelings. External circumstances merely trigger pleasant and unpleasant inner feelings. Buddha taught that we are of our own making and experiences, that we are "heir to deeds (karma); for deeds are the matrix, deeds are the kin, deeds are the foundation; whatever one does, good or bad, one will become heir to that." In Tibetan Buddhism it is taught that the eight worldly winds, or concerns, keep ordinary beings spinning around on the merry-go-round of conditioning: pleasure, pain, loss, gain, fame, shame, praise and criticism. Due to our reactivity and susceptibility to their distracting siren's call, these eight pitfalls are like currents uncontrollably blowing us hither and yon, exerting a profound influence over our human behavior through karmic cause and effect.

External circumstances can trigger various feelings, depending on which of our "buttons" get pushed and how wired (conditioned) we are to react; they are not the source of feelings, any more than a faucet is the source of tap water or cartons are the source of milk—the kind of misconceptions a young child is likely to have. There are no unequivocally positive or negative external things, events, feelings, or experiences—merely wanted and unwanted ones. Our experience is entirely subjective. Our mind channels how we experience reality and unreality through the mechanism of karmic interdependence and interconnectedness, a kind of spiritually helpful, karmically astute, general systems theory.

A learned old Tibetan lama once said, "The problem with you Westerners is that you mistake the primary causes of happiness and satisfaction for the secondary causes, thinking that happiness comes from outside." He meant that we mistakenly think that the hot button (which is merely the secondary cause) is the primary cause, while in actuality the primary cause is the reservoir of karma accumulated through our own prior actions, intentions, thoughts, and reactions, which condition us to subjectively react in certain habitual ways. The momentary event or other person we react to is merely the secondary cause, which turns on the tap's flow. The event or person is not the source of the water itself.

In general, there are three main kinds of karma: good (positive) karma, which involves virtuous activity; bad (negative) karma, which involves non-virtuous activity/vice; and neutral karma, which involves indeterminate or uncertain activity. Some actions or reactions are more heavily conditioned than others, so some are considered primary or definite causes. Others have lesser karmic weight and charge; therefore there are lesser causes for similar reactions and related implications to occur. In his book *Awakening through Love*, my colleague and friend Lama John Makransky provides an example of such differences in conditioning: "Beryl, my wife's mother, is a deeply loving person. When with her, I've noticed that if someone acts in a way that others would consider rude, she tends not to be upset by it. If a man callously pushes ahead of her in line at a cafeteria, instead of getting angry, Beryl might wonder if the man is feeling okay. 'Perhaps he has low blood sugar and needs to get food quickly,' she might say. If someone else, annoyed with him, suggests that he's just rude, Beryl will express compassion for him, saying something like, 'How difficult it must be to go through life in such a rush.' In Buddhist terms, because she has not been rude to others, Beryl doesn't know from the inside what its like to callously push others aside. So she tends not to take others' rude actions personally enough to feel the hurt and anger that others feel."

The law of karmic causation helps illuminate the universality of interconnectedness, interdependence, contingency and dependent origination. Karma increases and proliferates itself through reinforcing habitual tendencies and recreating familiar patterns. Each impulse we have lays down an imprint and, with repetition, becomes a groove. The groove creates a channel, and energy starts to be pulled in that direction. Once a groove is established, it can wear deeper with further repetition and habituation, becoming hard to change. This is how thoughts and intentions become actions, which lead to habitual patterns, which harden into personality and character traits and help create our individual destinies.

The bad news is that we're stuck with what we've done. The good news is that even the strongest habits and patterns are matters of repetition and conditioning, so they can be reconditioned—consciously, intelligently, and effectively. Even the deepest rut, such as addiction or brainwashing from cult mind control techniques, can gradually be graded, leveled, and smoothed out, according to the principles of karmic causation. One definition of insanity that I like is the tendency to keep doing the same thing over and over again while expecting better results. It should be obvious that if we want different results, we should do things differently. Our persistence in holding our past karmic actions in mind and memory can also be reconditioned and reframed—in a way, we can alter even our past.

Many people misunderstand the law of karma and think that it's purely a personal matter. When they witness someone suffering misfortune, they silently think, "You must have done something in the past or in a previous life that has produced this sad result." This kind of sloppy thinking can lead to the mistake of blaming the victim, as if it is entirely the crack baby's fault that he or she is born with an addiction, or the tsunami victims' fault that they lose their flooded homes and fields. The complex, interwoven, mysterious skein of karma is very difficult to understand.

The historical Buddha himself explained that one would have to be omniscient to understand the myriad karmas (or causative karmic actions and related factors) that produce even a single color on a single peacock's tail feather. The venerable Vietnamese Zen master Thich Nhat Han has characterized this as "interbeing," the interwoven karmic process involving plants, animals, nations, individuals, groups, and the world itself. The fact that people—and animals, too—undergo suffering as result of negative karma is the Buddha's teaching, yet this does not mean we can simplistically leap to the conclusion that people are to blame for the results of their karma and thus deserve what they get. The fact is that *everyone* experiences a vast interplay of forces that come to bear on what happens to them. No one stands apart from it or is in a position to judge others. Once we fundamentally understand this, we can begin to empathize and develop heartfelt compassion for everyone who is undergoing misery and difficulties, while learning how to improve our own karma and to skillfully cut through it to freedom and liberation for the sake of all.

It is important to realize there are different varieties of karma. There is individual karma, which is physical, emotional, personal, in which it is said that the results ripen solely upon the doer. An example is instant karma, where we do something foolish, clumsy, or inattentive and immediately experience the result. Beyond individual karma are family karma, collective karma, group karma, national karma, species karma, local karma, global karma, and so on. Americans, Japanese, dinosaurs, dolphins, and dodos all have different sorts of karma, related to their longstanding habits and patterns. The dinosaurs ruled the world for many millions of years and eventually became extinct, not because one dino was naughty, but because of species karma and global karma. Another example of group karma is the disproportionately large percentage of women getting breast cancer on Long Island. This statistical phenomenon is definitely not recurring simply because one woman or a thousand-plus women acted in such and such a way and thus deserve breast cancer. Rather, it's a combination of the group, the place, the society, the water, the air, the biochemicals—all factors in the Long Island women's karma, as distinct from (yet not entirely unrelated to) New Jersey women's karma or Long Island men's karma.

Karma should be understood as a complex nexus combining responsibility and the power and freedom of agency. The Buddha regarded the law of karma as an experientially self-evident principle, and he defined karmic action's formative factors as root, motive, volition, and intention. This is why Buddhist teachers always say that everything rests on the tip of intention or motivation. The fact is that greedy, self-centered, possessive, hateful intentions and actions inevitably lead, sooner or later, to unhappy results and further obscurations, while virtuous intention and unselfish actions inevitably lead to happy results and can further empower the potential to awaken. The Dalai Lama writes, "Buddha's teaching is that pleasure and pain arise from virtuous and non-virtuous actions which come not from outside, but from within yourself."

Ethical morality is not meant to be like a scourge to whip us sinners. It is a guide and a pole star to guide us towards better, more sane, harmonious, sensible, and happily fulfilled living. The better we understand the underlying laws and principles governing events and our reactions to them and interpretations of them, the better chance we have of living the love-filled lives we might actually want and choose to lead. Through understanding, we can avoid looking for what we want and need in the wrong places, repeating the same actions while hoping for and even expecting different results, and seeking happiness in ways which simply perpetuate our unhappiness and suffering.

A karma (action or result) always attains fruition in a way that is similar to the original act performed. This is called the similarity between the act and the result. Apple seeds do not produce lemon trees, although it must also be understood that apple seeds alone do not produce apple trees; a congeries of various other factors must also come together. We can learn how to become Dharma farmers instead of randomly sowing seeds hither and yon and later wondering why we and our family are hungry. For instance, if we seek happiness and fulfillment, our actions, thoughts, and intentions need to be consciously and intelligently directed to skillfully produce the actual intended results—through conscious cultivation of virtuous states of mind and heart. We must refrain from simply continuing to look for enduring love and satisfaction in all the wrong places while expecting better outcomes to ensue, as if by magic. Isn't it insane to continue doing what doesn't work in the hope that eventually it will?

When asked about past lives, Tibetan master Padma Sambhava said, "If you want to know your past life, look into your present condition; if you want to know your future life, look at your present action." In other words, we can grasp the steering wheel of life by more consciously and intelligently taking hold of our karma and understanding what is skillful and unskillful, helpful and harmful, virtue and vice. This is like Solomon's legendary God-given wisdom concerning discerning right from wrong. Buddha himself taught us to eschew the ten negative actions which produce bad karma:

- Killing

- Lying

- Stealing

- Sexual misconduct

- Intoxication

- Harsh and divisive speech

- Meaningless chatter

- Covetousness

- Evil intent

- Mistaken views

It is said that in order for the full effect of the negative karma from negative actions to occur, the negative action has to have four completed parts: is done intentionally; is accomplished and completed; is not regretted and repented; is not atoned for with vows or resolutions not to repeat such an act, which deter and put an end to repetitive karma. Without these four completed parts, negative karma can much more easily be transformed. If we sincerely feel regret and repentance for some past act, that alone helps lift some of the karmic burden.

Can karma be expiated, relieved, lessened, or even transferred? Karma is definite, yes; and although no one else can easily take it on for us—though there are many miracle stories to the contrary, in the literature as well as in oral lore—karma can be lessened, expiated, transformed, purified and destroyed; and there are numerous ways and means to do so. How? Through antidotes, such as through any appropriate virtuous activity intentionally dedicated towards purifying karma—such as saving lives by freeing animals, or retooling stinginess and attachment by giving more, without expectation of return. Helping out those who we feel have harmed or slighted us can greatly recondition habitual reactions such as attachment, bitterness, and aversion. Throughout history many repentant great sinners have become purified saints and sages, such as the Tibetan yogimaster Milarepa, and Buddha's disciple, the former serial killer Angulimala, through this skillful path of transformative spiritual awakening and personal redemption. My Tibetan teachers recommend six antidotes for purifying karma:

1. Reading, reproducing, and sharing sacred scriptures and wise words of the masters

2. Meditating on the true nature of reality, such as Buddha's four basic facts of life: impermanence, selflessness, emptiness/illusoriness, and moving beyond conceptual reification

3. Chanting mantras and prayers, particularly purification mantras

4. Presenting and disseminating sacred knowledge and awakened art

5. Giving generously to and altruistically helping those in need

6. Reciting lineage prayers and praises in gratitude and reverent appreciation

Buddhism teaches that no matter what we did in the past, we determine our own future and can do so with more conscious intentionality. Buddha said, "No one can defile or purify another." Yet Buddhist masters feel it is important to understand that, above all, karma is pliable and malleable, and help can be applied from outside as well as from within. Teachings, explanations, encouragement, modeling, and instructions can all help us work toward changing, steering, and transforming our karma. How we may wisely do so is one of the most important questions and teachings of enlightened wisdom.

We are each responsible for our lives and our experience of

them. As I always say, it's not what happens, but what we make of it that makes all the difference. It's not just the cards that we are dealt, but how we play the game that determines its outcome. My teacher once said, "People are led by karma. A Bodhisattva (an Awakener, a Wisdom Warrior, a Buddha-to be) is skillful in being able to steer his own karma." This is why awakening and transforming ourselves transforms our world and is ultimately of interest and relevance to everyone. The most important thing I want to say about karma is that we can grab hold of the rudders and oars of our lives. We can't control the prevailing winds, but we can certainly learn how to sail and navigate better. We are masters rather than victims, and we can steer our karma, transforming our karma (reactivity and conditioning) into our Dharma (enlightened living). Everything rests on the tip of intention. It is said in one of the Buddhist sutras:

> *With good intention upon entering a foreign temple,*
> *One man placed*
> *His boots*
> *On Buddha's head.*
> *Another, equally well-intentioned,*
> *Took them off.*
> *And both*
> *Were later reborn as kings.*

7

*One instant of total awareness is one instant of perfect freedom
and enlightenment.*

—FROM THE *SONG OF ONE THOUSAND NAMES OF MANJUSRI*

What is Enlightenment?

Enlightenment is not what you think it is. It's not something
our intellect can grasp. Of course, that doesn't stop us from
conceptualizing it, and our concepts about it can serve a beneficial, temporary purpose. They can help inspire and direct our
quest for enlightenment, even if words can't fully describe it.
Enlightenment means spiritual illumination, realization, freedom, and the ultimate actualization of all that we are and can
be. First and foremost, however, I feel obliged to emphasize that
we must never confuse the map—in this case, our concepts
about enlightenment—with the actual territory. Nirvana, or
enlightenment, is not what we think it is, nor is it otherwise—
to put it in Zen-speak. A Buddhist secret is that you just can't

believe everything you think! If you think you understand God or heaven, Buddha or nirvana, please reconsider; try to look further into these deep matters. Enlightenment is like being spiritually reborn, within this very life—a very particular kind of rebirth, however, not merely as a person of renewed and reinvigorated faith, but as one fully endowed with all the characteristics and ideal qualities of a selfless and loving saint, a wise and compassionate sage.

In the Tibetan language, the word for enlightenment (jang-chub) means full awakening, total purification, and an utterly complete blossoming and unfolding of primordial awareness-wisdom and unconditional love. Thus the Asian symbol of enlightenment is often the lotus, a dazzlingly fresh, unsullied flower that emerges through murky mud and water to unfold its shining petals in the light of day. Spiritual enlightenment is the pearl beyond price, more valuable than gold and jewels. Like the blossoming lotus flower, or the pearl found within an oyster; what we seek is within each and every one of us and not to be found, acquired, or obtained anew from elsewhere. The lotus is our own innate potential, simply awaiting recognition, unfolding, and actualization. Recognizing who and what we truly are is the secret of realizing authentic enlightenment.

Buddhism is basically a religion of enlightenment, a wisdom tradition rather than a faith, creed, or belief system. Its sole goal, regardless of which country it's found in, is enlightenment. The Sanskrit word that Buddhists habitually translate as "enlightenment" is *bodhi*, which literally means to awaken. It is the root of the term that Buddha used to describe himself: When asked if he was a god, a saint, a guru, a wizard, an avatar, or an angel, he replied, "I am an awakened one, a Buddha." From what does an enlightened being wake up? From the sleep of ignorance and delusion, confusion and suffering. To what does he or she awaken? To an authentically greater life of truth, clarity, freedom, peace, and deathless bliss, as Buddha himself described it: a full awareness of who and what one is and one's true place in this world.

Enlightenment is precisely what the historical sage now known as the Buddha experienced twenty-five hundred years ago when he sat down to meditate beneath a fig tree in northern India, vowing to remain there until he either resolved the fundamental mystery of life, death, and the universe or his body turned to dust. After he achieved the former spiritual breakthrough, he quickly became renowned as a wise and compassionate teacher of multitudes. Without a doubt, individuals before the Buddha had attained varieties of extraordinary states of mind-body consciousness, like spiritual realization, oneness with God, inner illumination, bliss. Yet until the Buddha achieved full enlightenment beneath that fig tree, no one we know about in history had ever awakened in quite the way he did. Buddha discovered enlightenment, as most Easterners conceive of it. His peerless awakening is termed *samyak sambodhi* in Sanskrit: no mere, fleeting spiritual epiphany, but complete and irreversible, supreme enlightenment—entry into deathless nirvana. Afterward, he generously offered the world his own road map to nirvana, the Noble Eightfold Path—the way to enlightenment and the steps of enlightened living.

All Buddhist traditions offer a tried and true path of awakening and enlightenment. Enlightenment experience in the ancient Theravadin Buddhist tradition is traditionally developed through the four gradual stages of purification known as:

- Stream Enterer (one who glimpses reality, the unconditioned nature of things)

- Once Returner (one who has progressed in spiritual development to the point where he or she can achieve enlightenment in one more lifetime)

- None Returner (one who requires no more rebirths)

- Arhat (a selfless saint liberated from the cycle of birth and death)

One progresses along this path by developing penetrating insight into universal facts: the impermanence and unreliability of all that is; the selfless, hollow, insubstantial nature of things and beings; and the dissatisfactory nature of all conditioned things, which cannot in the long run provide true fulfillment and contentment. In Mahayana Buddhism, enlightenment begins when a Bodhisattva, or unselfish spiritual seeker, first experiences sunyata, the luminous void-emptiness—oneness and selflessness—that is the fundamental characteristic or true nature of all and everything. Japanese Buddhists call it *satori*—literally, breakthrough: a naked glimpse of nothingness. Masters say that this breakthrough is the beginning of the ultimate path, not the end of it. From there the Bodhisattva ascends through the ten *bhumis* (stages) of the ladder to enlightenment until reaching perfect and supreme enlightenment, known as Buddhahood, the ultimate goal of all Buddhist traditions.

A spiritual revolutionary and world changer, the enlightened Buddha taught that anyone can become enlightened, whether old or young, learned or illiterate, male or female—and, I believe, Buddhist or otherwise. In doing so, he challenged India's rigid, age-old caste system and patriarchy, saying that enlightenment is the birthright of everyone, part and parcel of our innate being, not something that we have to seek outside or something anyone can give us. We are all Buddhas by nature, as the tantric texts remind us. Our only spiritual task is to recognize and awaken to that fact. Unfortunately, most of us are usually sleeping Buddhas rather than energetic, awakened ones. That is the problem, spiritually speaking.

Fully awakening in this manner means realizing who and what we truly are, apart from the myriad, transitory worldly identities we build, acquire, imagine, cling to, and suffer from. Millions have fulfilled the promise of enlightenment by awakening to this inner realization. The awakened have fulfilled the promise of enlightenment, a vital aspect of which is becoming aware for the first time that we are inseparable from everyone and everything else in the universe: that all are totally interconnected, in a state that the Zen teacher Thich Nhat Han calls "interbeing." This awareness leads spontaneously to genuine feelings of selfless love and unconditional compassion and compels us towards universal responsibility and altruistic service. The Twelfth Gyalwang Drukpa Rinpoche says, "Enlightenment can only be achieved through understanding your own nature—the nature of universal truth that is within yourself. That kind of total understanding or enlightenment takes the form of active love and compassion."

To me, the enlightened state of mind is one of buoyant, incandescent clarity coupled with authentic, transparent presence. Enlightenment is the evolution of consciousness beyond the illusion that one has a separate existence. It's a realization that transcends mind and body, yet includes both of them, as well as all and everything else. It is a maturation of our innate awareness that leads beyond immaturity, dependence, gullibility, delusion, confusion, misperceptions, and misknowing. This inner realization, or illumination, opens into the ultimate form of direct, trans-conceptual seeing, what Buddhists call Clear Vision and Wise Knowing, by means of which we perceive things just as they truly are. This is the wisdom of Awareness.

These days it seems easier to get awakened than to stay awakened, and there are many ways to do so. But having a religious or spiritual experience is not as significantly meaningful as actually developing and sustaining a religious and spiritual life. That is one problem with special peak experiences: However extraordinary they may be, they are fleeting. Unless we learn how to progress from such experiences into a sustained, ever-deepening spiritual life, they soon fade from our memory, until they're essentially forgotten.

Enlightenment can present itself very quickly, such as in a sudden peak experience or epiphany, but more often it's a gradual process. It's an opening up to greater and greater freedom and harmony as we come ever closer to a compassionate, all-embracing wisdom that surpasses common understanding. Tibetan texts say that total enlightenment has five characteristics: It is profound, tranquil, uncomplicated, luminous, and unfabricated (that is, not compounded of, or conditioned by, other things). In its depth and simplicity, enlightenment is like a vast, undisturbed, radiant, and infinitely empty openness.

Our evolutionary realization of enlightenment begins with the slow integration of our "empty" (selfless, immaterial, yet cognizant) and lucidly transparent mind—increasingly cleared of desires, expectations, and preconceptions—into the ordinary activities of our life. Our ego can and does still affect our behavior as we go through this process, but more and more of its manifestations are tamed, and its presence becomes increasingly irrelevant. Ordinary life continues to be problematic. After all, in the realm of samsara, or worldly things, everything is relative, with corresponding ups and downs. The difference is that as our realization of enlightenment deepens, we become less deluded by worldly pleasures and momentary appearances, thus less ensnared by reactivity and related difficulties.

The cultivation of an enlightened heart and mind through

mindfulness and self-inquiry is a practice that progressively leads us to abandon our fixation on possessing or conceptually knowing things—in other words, on permanence and certainty. Instead, we come to function on a higher, more dynamic level of not-attachment and not-knowing. In short, we learn the true art of living, the practice of freedom, the art of authentic *being*. As the contemporary spiritual teacher Eckhart Tolle once said, "Enlightenment means choosing to dwell in the state of presence rather than in time. It means saying yes to what is."

Buddhists define the wisdom of enlightenment as that which perfectly understands both essence and manifestation, knowing exactly how things fundamentally are, as well as how they appear and function. They believe it is a transcendental insight that is inseparable from selfless love and compassion. There are said to be many degrees and levels of enlightenment and different depths and characteristics of the various enlightenment experiences. Each experience opens us up to greater degrees of freedom, unconditional love, and radiant wisdom.

Even if we do wake up to enlightenment in an irreversible, unshakeable, forceful, and cosmic way, as the historical Buddha did, bringing enlightenment to life is a never-ending endeavor. It is also a cooperative venture, as opposed to an individual enterprise. Enlightenment is, in the literal sense of the English word, "bringing light" to a dark, benighted world. It involves refining a state of consciousness that transcends the narrow limits of self and expands to encompass the universe. In terms of Mahayana Buddhism, the entire purpose of striving to become enlightened and to lead an enlightened life is to serve all sentient beings, because, in fact, we're all in the same boat, and "others" are none other than ourselves. We need each other, as the Dalai Lama says. Compassion and empathy are necessary to achieve enlightenment, and other beings are the proximate cause for the rise of those highly positive and noble spiritual emotions.

Stories about enlightenment experiences abound. My favorite collections of them are *Zen Flesh, Zen Bones* by Paul Reps and the various biographies of Buddhist masters such as Milarepa, Marpa, and Shabkar Rinpoche, which are chock full of spontaneous songs of enlightenment (called *dohas*) and inspiring and edifying teaching tales. My own published collection of traditional Tibetan teaching tales told by my masters, *The Snow Lion's Turquoise Mane: Wisdom Tales from Tibet*, contains many such stories.

Audacious people sometimes ask me if I, as a spiritual teacher and a representative of a Buddhist lineage, am enlightened. I have sometimes heard myself say, "Enlightened enough—for now!" I will stand by that. I can live with that, while I continue my journey—being there while getting there, every single step of the way. The truth is that today I think a lot less about grandiose, idealistic goals such as enlightenment, and simply live more at ease in this marvelous moment, the present moment, where the action really is.

Buddhism is an inside job. When I become clear, everything is clear. With enlightenment, everything changes, yet nothing changes; we discover what has been there all along, obscured by our conflicting passions, emotions, illusions, and attachments. Transforming oneself transforms the world. To save one soul is to save the whole world. No one can do all the good that the world needs, but the world needs all the good that you and I can do.

8

The more we have made our lives meaningful, the less we will regret at the time of death. The way we feel when we come to die is thus very dependent on the way we have lived.

—THE DALAI LAMA

*Even death is nothing to fear
For those who have lived wisely.*

—THE BUDDHA

What Happens After Death?

Death is the most important question of our time, according to eminent psychologist Robert Lifton. Everyone must wonder about their own demise at sometime during their lifetime. The scientifically minded Dalai Lama says that he is very interested in seeing what happens when he goes through the process of dying and looks forward to it like an experiment. No one wants to die, yet everyone must. Is there an after-life? Most of us want to believe that there is some continuity to our existence and that we don't face total oblivion after our bodies cease to function. Thus the old adage: To the unbeliever, death is the end; to the believer, the beginning.

Perhaps this seemingly built-in will-to-believe is, in itself, some slight evidence that existence does go on. The key problem in addressing the question of death is that our rational minds—limited to working within our finite, worldly mode of being—can't penetrate the mysteries of exactly *how*, where, and in what precise form life continues. Moreover, few and far between are those who return from beyond the pale to inform and update us. How then shall we prepare ourselves better to face death and eternity? Does anyone know for a fact what, if anything, goes on beyond this life?

In Freud's time, sex and death were unmentionable topics in polite society. Historian Arnold Toynbee joked that death is un-American, referring to our optimistic, youth-oriented nature. A Buddhist joke says that it is easier to die than to stay dead. (This refers to the cycle of rebirth.) Oscar Wilde quipped that "One can survive anything these days except death." Religions throughout human history have evolved supra-rational cosmologies, teachings, rituals, practices, and articles of faith concerning what happens to us after death, intending to help us overcome the considerable limitations of our logical thinking in order to better confront, and eventually resolve for ourselves, questions about death and its consequences. Otherwise, we can't help but wonder about, worry about, and, ultimately, fear losing the mortal life we have. Therefore, it's important for each of us to explore and develop our own ideas on the subject and then to investigate further what other, possibly more compelling, ideas are possible. Simply to avoid the subject or be close-minded about it leaves us wide open to unnecessary, often unconscious, fears and suffering. We may also wind up surprisingly and woefully ill prepared for the critical moment of death when it inevitably arrives, not to mention its aftermath.

Why do we die? The definitive answer is because we are born. Without birth, no death, whether a beggar or a king, a saint, a pet, a fly. Yet we hardly think about it in that way, for various reasons—perhaps primary among them is that we take life for granted and regard death as an imposition. "Death is a Dialogue between the Spirit and the Dust," as Emily Dickinson sang. In fact, death is necessary for Mother Nature's lovely seasons to turn and for the generations to progress and evolve. Befriending death is in our own higher self-interest, as it is undeniably a part—even a major part—of life. If our society shuts us away from the facts of death, and ageing, illness, and other facts of life, and protects us from awareness of the unpleasant aspects of existence, I believe that in the long run this state of denial is to our collective and personal detriment.

Tibetan Buddhism is widely acknowledged among religious scholars to have one of the most highly developed systems of thanatology, the science of death and dying. It has helped spawn the modern hospice movement. A Tibetan saying has it that there is no better gift one can give than to help someone die well. Tibetan wisdom on this recondite subject is embodied for common use in the renowned Buddhist classic, *Bardo Thodol* (*The Tibetan Book of Guidance for the Dead*), which is most accessible to Westerners in Sogyal Rinpoche's popular condensed version, *The Tibetan Book of Living and Dying.* The *Bardo Thodol* explains how to use our human life as preparation for the art of dying, combining both theory and practice. In this text, Buddhism teaches us how to rehearse for death—for example while falling asleep each night, known as "the small death." Also taught is lucid dreaming—mindfully practicing waking up within dreams and recognizing you are dreaming, while still remaining asleep—and other techniques of conscious mastery over experience within dreams, bringing insightful lessons which carry over into experience within the daydream of life. These insights also help us continue to practice conscious, wakeful living right up to and throughout the moment of death, and even beyond into the intermediate stage between death and rebirth known as *bardo.* We learn to recognize and follow the clear light of spirit—to focus on the inner light, to be and become the light—beyond fear or desire, whatever form it may take.

My friend Gehlek Rinpoche, in his book *Good Life, Good Death*, writes, "Death is like sleep. Bardo is like a dream between death and another life. Then you wake up. . . . The best thing to prepare yourself for death is to practice patience, love and compassion in your daily life and keep a watch on ego." In the *Bardo Thodol,* we are specifically instructed on how to guide oneself (as a practitioner), or assist the mind-stream and energy of a deceased person, through the dissolution of the five elements of the physical body into consciousness itself, and then into the clear light of the inner nature of mind. This prepares us to better recognize and understand the hallucinatory sights and sounds, shapes and colors, of the interlife transition and proceed unhindered onwards and upwards on the evolutionary cycle of rebirth towards more highly elevated development. We learn how to recognize the clear light of reality, first, at the moment of death; second, in the intermediate stage (bardo), or transitional passage between this life and the next (rebirth), in order to be able to transform our basic consciousness into primordial enlightened mind; and third, ultimately become liberated from the vicious cycle of unconscious conditioning and delusion at the root of samsara (the bonds of cyclic existence) by consciously choosing whether or not, where, and in what form to be reborn in this world.

The *Bardo Thodol* teachings instruct us how both to live and die well—which means consciously, with full awareness, clarity, and intention. Thus we discover the meaning and purpose of our lives and do not go empty-handed, alone and afraid, into the murky passageways beyond this finite world and this mortal life. As the French essayist Michel de Montaigne said, "To practice death is to practice freedom. A man who has learned how to die has unlearned how to be a slave." *The Medieval Christian Book of the Art of Dying* says, "Learn to die and thou shalt learn how to live. There shall none learn how to live that hath not learned how to die." The moment of death provides a unique opportunity for spiritual experience and internal transformation and exaltation.

Christianity teaches that people who are good in this life are rewarded with an eternal, blissful existence in heaven, while evil people are condemned to never-ending torment in hell. For some, including Roman Catholics, there's a state of purgatory in between, where, among other things, people on the borderline between good or bad serve temporary—sometimes extremely long—penance before being admitted to heaven. Jews likewise believe in a heaven for good people, if not in a hell for bad ones. Muslims have faith in a merit-based heaven as well as a demerit-based hell. Hindus, Jains, Buddhists, Sikhs, and Taoists, by way of contrast, believe in some form of reincarnation (in which the soul or "individual self" is reborn into another body) or rebirth (our present life affects the quality of a subsequent life, although little personal imprint is carried over). In the case of either reincarnation or rebirth, one's relative virtue or vice, attachments, attractions, aversions, and level of consciousness determine the next kind of life that occurs.

Religious people often ask me if there is really a heaven and hell, and if we are accountable in some form of afterlife for our actions here today and tomorrow. My short answer is yes, I have seen this. But the truth is that heaven and hell are not what we *think* they are. They assume various forms and guises. They are not permanent states of ultimate existence, yet they do sometimes seem to carry the claustrophobic illusion of being interminably long-lasting. I know you're wondering how I can know this, and I don't expect you to take my word for it, nor should you. My inner certainty and conviction come through meditation and Tibetan Dream Yoga's lucid dreaming practice; other fruitful methods could include intense holotropic breathing training,

Jungian dream work, out-of-body experiences, psychic awareness development, rebirthing and so forth—all tools and techniques available in today's burgeoning spiritual marketplace.

I personally think that many, if not most, of our ideas about heaven and hell, in this life as well as the afterlife, are culturally conditioned beliefs and concepts, rather than universally applicable truths. Whether or not we subscribe to any particular cultural tradition or religious system, how we live, think, and understand things greatly affects our after-death experience. Furthermore, I'd guess that our untrammeled innate spiritual nature, whatever we may call it, precedes and postdates our own birth and death, and that this luminous mental energy or intrinsic nature of heart-mind continues in one form or another, immaterial and transpersonal as it may be. This is the basis of the Eastern thought traditions regarding reincarnation. For me, this intuitively feels right. Check this out yourself.

Stories told in the Tibetan *de-lok* tradition by those who have, as it were, returned from the beyond (the literal meaning of the word de-lok) are similar in many ways to what modern science has termed near-death experiences. Such individuals have encountered bright lights, cacophonous sounds, angelic beings, and visions both beneficent and horrific. These individuals, including Chakdud Tulku Rinpoche's late mother, have regaled us with cautionary tales about the inevitable results of karmic actions, confirmed by their encounters with deceased people formerly known to them whom they met again in the shadowy afterworld.

The common denominator in virtually all representations of the after-life or other lives is that we go on to some type of existence where we reap the results of our moral and spiritual behavior during this life. If you believe in a higher truth or power at all, whether theistic or karmic, it makes metaphysical sense that this is the way things work. The many different forms in which humans have imagined post-death existence, various as they are, all point to this pattern. By definition, it's beyond our capacity to describe or understand completely, so we often simply talk around the mystery and leave it unexamined.

Lying beneath a tree in Kushinagar, the historical Buddha, at age eighty, before taking his last breath and entering parinirvana (nirvana after death), advised us to regard the transience of life and work out our salvation with diligence. Many Tibetan lamas, including the Tibetan leaders renowned as the Dalai Lama and the high-ranking Karmapa Lama, are famous for their ability to choose their next reincarnation and then indicate it to their successors. This skill allows their reincarnated Bodhisattva wisdom-mind to be found embodied in youthful form. Once returned to their monastic seat, they can continue their careers as Bodhisattvas (enlightened wisdom masters who remain in the cycle of birth-and-death to assist others to become enlightened). Even today, the Tibetan reincarnated-lama, or *tulku*, system is important in maintaining spiritual and cultural institutions, as well as the intact lineage of transmitted teachings and initiations, among Tibetans the world over.

The late Sixteenth Karmapa, my own guru, was widely renowned for his prodigious psychic powers and abilities. Through his clairvoyance and predictive powers, he definitively recognized and enthroned hundreds of tulkus (reincarnate lamas), helping to maintain the Tibetan Vajrayana tradition intact throughout the world outside old Tibet. Some of these tulkus (also called "Golden Children" or "Living Buddhas") have told me that they could remember their previous lives. Others have said that as they grew up, their past-life recollections faded as new, present-life impressions accumulated. For years it was difficult for me to accept such stories or even believe in rebirth, not to mention reincarnation. As I became more and more familiar with youthful tulkus during my decades in India and the Himalayas, I was finally convinced. There was no other explanation for what these very sincere, honest, wise, and quite credible human beings said they could recall, or for their remarkable level of spiritual accomplishment at such young ages. They were obviously Mozart-like spiritual prodigies.

A firm belief in rebirth or reincarnation goes far to eliminate the fears human beings normally hold about death. My first lama, Thubten Yeshe, in Nepal, who had been diagnosed with a possibly fatal heart murmur, told me on several occasions during the 1970s that he wasn't afraid of dying. He had died so many times already, he claimed, that there was no uncertainty left to fear. He knew he'd be back among the living soon afterward, he told me. Just imagine his followers' delight when, after dying in his late forties during the 1980s, the Dalai Lama recognized his reincarnation as the fifth and youngest son of two of his Spanish disciples! I'll admit that I was a little skeptical at first. But the well-known Buddhist scholar and agnostic Stephen Batchelor and I visited the Spanish-born tulku one day, and came away shaking our heads in wonderment. The little boy reminded us both very much of the insouciant Lama Yeshe we had each known and loved in the 1970s.

Not all enlightened people become intentionally and consciously reincarnated beings. Different schools of Buddhism discuss various other forms of rebirth—different possibilities for next-life existence—including versions of heaven and hell that are not associated with permanent states of being, but, instead, with temporary lifetimes. Most Mahayana Buddhists believe there are six temporary realms of existence into which we can be reborn, based on the good or bad karma (actions and reactions) we generate before we die. From the lowest realm to the highest in terms of comfort, they are: hellish creatures (totally miserable), hungry ghosts (craving insatiably), animals (concerned only with bodily demands), humans (still suffering, but capable of self-conscious reflection and enlightenment), demi-gods (asuras, powerful but belligerent), and gods (devas, long-lived, proud and happy yet still subject to eventual deterioration and death).

When the Tibetan-born lama Chogyam Trungpa Rinpoche taught in the Western world—one of the first Tibetan lamas to do so—he often explained these six realms of existence as symbolic of psychological states of being, each of which we can experience occasionally during a single human lifetime. This doesn't preclude them from also being realms into which we are reborn, but Trungpa Rinpoche skillfully chose to fit his message to his audience; he knew that Europeans and Americans without culture-supported belief in rebirth and reincarnation needed another way to approach the whole idea. When teaching in Tibet, from which he was exiled during the Chinese Communist takeover of the 1950s, he usually focused on the more traditional life-cycle aspect of the six realms.

Tibetan lamas also teach about the Pure Lands, or Buddhafields, rarefied paradisiacal states of existence outside the six realms, yet not quite the same as nirvana itself. Once reborn into one of those celestial dimensions or subtle energy-fields, beings can more easily progress toward enlightenment, free from many of the shackles of suffering and karma associated with human life. An entire school of Buddhism, called the Pure Land School, especially popular in Japan, which exists also throughout Asia and even the United States, is based on praying to be reborn in Buddha Amitabha's Pure Land of Great Bliss. In my opinion, such pure lands or Buddhafields are roughly comparable to the devout Christian's concept of heaven, though certainly not identical.

When asked in recent years, "What is the nature of the mindstream that reincarnates from lifetime to lifetime?", the Dalai Lama said, "If one understands the term 'soul' as a continuum of individuality from moment to moment, from lifetime to lifetime, then one can say that Buddhism also accepts a concept of soul; there is a kind of continuum of consciousness. From that point of view, the debate on whether or not there is a soul becomes strictly semantic. However, in the Buddhist doctrine of selflessness or 'no soul' theory, the understanding is that there is no eternal, unchanging, abiding, permanent (separate) self called 'soul.' . . . Buddhism does not deny the continuum of consciousness. We find diverse opinions, even among Buddhist scholars, as to what exactly the nature of self is, what exactly that thing or entity is that continues from one moment to the next moment, from one lifetime to the next lifetime." (From *Healing Anger: The Power of Patience from a Buddhist Perspective* by the Dalai Lama, translated by Geshe Thupten Jinpa.)

Why should it be any more surprising or unfathomable that we have many lives rather than just one? Psychologist Carl Jung, Freud's prominent disciple, believed in rebirth, enumerating and defining five different yet related types in his 1939 essay, "Concerning Rebirth." They are metempsychosis, reincarnation, resurrection, rebirth within one life, and transformation. Other thinkers have used terms such as the transmigration of souls, palingenesis, re-embodiment, and future life. Icons of modern thought and literature including Leo Tolstoy, Thomas Edison, Ralph Waldo Emerson, Henry David Thoreau, Albert Schweitzer, and Mahatma Gandhi all believed in reincarnation. Socrates, the father of Western philosophy, believed in reincarnation as logically explained in his last discourse in Plato's *Phaedo*. Who remembers that, prior to the Council of Nicea in 325 A.D., Christians believed in reincarnation? It was only then that this popular doctrine was struck from the orthodox canon by church theologians. Nevertheless, many Westerners continue to believe in some form of the afterlife today, and even as many as 30 percent of Americans believe in reincarnation (according to recent polls), although 85 percent say they believe in some form of an afterlife. Regarding rebirth, Buddhism reminds us to notice through lucid mindfulness that death and rebirth take place not just after we die and go through the various stages of bardo, but also in every moment. With each breath and with each flickering of consciousness, the old dies and the new is born, in connection with and dependent upon, but not identical to, what went before.

Is there anything observable in nature at either its macro or micro levels that simply arises out of nothing, uncaused, and disappears again without outflow or effect? Isn't almost everything cyclical, interconnected, and functioning through an immense and subtle skein of interwoven causes and effects? I personally feel quite certain that there is some kind of subtle continuance to our lives. The most basic life philosphies recognize the old saw that what goes around comes around, which is nothing other than the ineluctable law of karma, and that we reap what we've sown. Even modern physics proposes laws which echo ancient Buddhist verities, such as the law of conservation of energy, which states energy can be neither created nor destroyed. But regarding our human existence: what exactly continues, and in what form, through what mechanism, with what possible margin of error—these questions remain open to further inquiry.

Once I asked a middle-aged lama friend of mine in Darjeeling if he was afraid of death or of the pain and uncertainty of dying. He said, "I am not afraid of death or dying. I am afraid of vice and of unconscious living." Because we can never "eff" the ineffability of death and its aftermath, we may find it tempting to ignore the whole issue. I believe in my heart, however, that we do so at our own peril. Buddha himself said that just as the footprint of the elephant is the largest in the jungle, to contemplate death and mortality is the greatest and most liberating of mindfulness meditations. When I first read that many years ago, at a young age, I thought it was a little morbid. But later I came to find out that keeping death in the forefront of consciousness helps us to face the facts of life, such as impermanence, change, and the insubstantiality and mysterious ungraspability of it all.

A keen sense of life's tenuous, evanescent nature helps us to let go a little; prioritize things in light of the fact that we won't be here forever; experience gratitude, reverence, and awe; and realize that we can ill afford to procrastinate regarding the most important matters and people. Such awareness helps us to cherish life and value time, energy, and the inconceivable magic of aliveness itself, rather than squandering it. Reflecting on life's lessons amidst change and uncertainty encourages the wisdom of experience, helping us prepare for our end by befriending death, rather than remaining in denial and being blindsided by sickness, aging, and death. "Learn as if you were going to live forever. Live as if you were going to die tomorrow," said

Mahatma Gandhi. In a sutra teaching given to seven daughters, Buddha said, "If one knows that what is born will end in death, then there will be love."

Intentionally considering one's own demise and the demise of loved ones acts as a catalyst to conscious evolution, providing insight into questions like: Where do we come from? What is our place in this world and this universe? Who lives? Who and what, exactly, dies? I urge you to consider these questions.

Here's how to start: Take solitary, unhurried, contemplative walks in local cemeteries. Read the inscriptions on the gravestones and reflect upon all those who have lived and loved, laughed and cried, given birth, parented and aged, come and gone—and remember that our lives and deaths follow a similar path. In doing this, I like to contemplate death, eternity, and my own finitude, along with the miracle and mystery that I am alive and functioning at all. I wonder, "What shall I do with this precious life right now?" Also, make it a practice to ask people you know whose lives and experience you especially value for their response to this question.

The Sufis I knew in my youth said, "Die before you die, and you shall never die." This refers to the need for ego-death, spiritual rebirth, and life eternal.

We are all going to die, of course, but who among us is truly going to *live*?

9

*Spiritual friends and lovingkindness are the
whole of the holy life.*

—THE BUDDHA

*We are not human beings having a spiritual experience.
We are spiritual beings having a human experience.*

—PIERRE TEILHARD DE CHARDIN, PHILOSOPHER

How Can I Integrate Spirituality into My Daily Life?

The story goes that one day Helen, an elementary school teacher, had her first grade class draw with pencils and crayons. She was walking around the classroom looking over her students' work—encouraging here, helping out there, enjoying and appreciating the entire show—when she came to little Camilla, who was furiously working on her picture. "What are you drawing, Camilla?" she asked. Camilla replied, "I'm drawing a picture of God."

"But Camilla," Helen said, "no one knows what God looks like." "They will in a minute!" exclaimed Camilla, and she got back to work. Camilla shows us the can-do, will-do, am-doing spirit of the intrepid spiritual seeker, the heroic wisdom warrior, little Buddha within—the Buddha to be.

It is difficult, if not impossible, for most of us to accomplish the great undertaking known as the spiritual journey by ourselves. It's too easy to stray off-course or fall into traps if we rely solely on our own limited, self-oriented point of view as we try to reinvent the wheel and create our own path. To help ensure that we see beyond ourselves, we need seeking companions and experienced helpmates, mentors, kind benefactors, and other sympathetic and supportive kindred spirits along the way.

How can joining an established religion or spiritual group help? How can you find the best match? Similar to choosing a vocation or health regimen, when choosing a path or tradition, it is helpful to be aware of one's own proclivities and inclinations—your spiritual personality type. Traditionally, in India, the many traditions are generally grouped into two: faith-based, or devotional-emotional (*bhakta*), and intellectual-philosophical, or knowledge-oriented (*jnana*). In Western thought, practitioners of the timeless traditions have generally been divided between contemplatives and good-deeds, service-oriented activists. Some people feel more spiritual, rather than strictly religious. Some of us are joiners. We seek and need the structure, security, continuity, kinship, and solace of communal rites and celebrations, of congregational religion and community activities.

Others are more individualistic, maverick, do-it yourself seekers. Some are more tolerant, inclusive, eclectic; others are more dogmatic, creed-oriented, or even exclusive.

These kinds of distinctions account for the varying emphases even within one tradition of different schools and sects (within Christianity, Judaism, or Hinduism, for example). While adhering to the teachings of one founder or set of founders, individuals may emphasize and practice different aspects of the religion. Politically speaking, every religion includes both extremists and fundamentalists, as well as more moderate adherents. However, in discerning which kind of spiritual path to follow, a more useful distinction might be between the traditional, preservation-oriented loyalists of any religion, on the one hand, and the progressives, reformers, and innovative free-thinking adherents of that same religious tradition, on the other.

For today, I would say there are six kinds of general personality types we could consider:

1. Heart-centered (devotional-emotional, faith-oriented)

2. Rational (intellectual-philosophical)

3. Spiritual (prayer and meditation-based)

4. Yogic (physical-energetic)

5. Ritual-based (musical and artistic)

6. Shamanistic (psychic-phenomena and healing oriented)

Most of us encompass aspects of all six types, although one or two of these predilections commonly predominate. Thus, we naturally find ourselves attracted to different kinds or styles of spiritual practice or worship on our way to spiritual literacy.

Faith, beautiful in its own way, is not without its dark side—the shadow face of blind faith that includes gullibility, follow-the-leader mentality, and even mass hysteria (such as in dangerous cults). There are both up- and down-sides to organized religions—and groups of all kinds, as any intelligent person must be aware of. Moreover, many Americans have trouble accepting the need for an organizational approach to spirituality. After all, it is deeply ingrained in our nature to be individualistic, egalitarian, and somewhat mistrustful of authority figures and large institutions.

In the early 1800s, founders of the Transcendental Movement included the American philosopher Ralph Waldo Emerson and several of his cohorts in Massachusetts, among them Henry David Thoreau. They called upon the individual to rise above established dogma and recognize eternal truths in his or her everyday life. In so doing, they initiated what the venerable literary critic Harold Bloom trenchantly terms the American Religion. Ever since Transcendentalism, Bloom maintains, our national style of religious seeking has been set, for better or worse, on the path of personal exploration rather than traditional practice. Traditional churches remain strong in this country, yet many of us choose not to follow a set of old beliefs. Instead, we demand a new, fresh, vibrant, and transformative personal spiritual experience. Even if we grant the value of this approach, however, I believe the question remains: What is the path to the kind of transformative experience we want? It's doubtful we can ever know without a little help from experienced friends, which brings us back to the notion of a group of like-minded seekers and trained teachers.

To begin engaging in your own search for a possible spiritual path to follow, start by asking yourself these questions:

What is my religion, at least on paper?

What do I believe in, if anything?

What did my parents and grandparents believe in? Are my beliefs the same, different, related?

How would the ideal religion for me actually look, feel, function?

What do I think I want out of my religion or spiritual path and practices?

What do I most like about my religion? Least?

Whom do I consider the most spiritually inspiring person (alive or dead)?

What are my favorite prayers, hymns, pieces of sacred music, artworks?

What style of worship or spiritual practice do I like best?

Is there one particular religion or spiritual tradition

besides my own that I might be interested in learning more about, for any reason?

What might happen if I pursued that religion?

People both within and outside of Buddhism often ask me how to strengthen their spirituality and bring it into daily life. I learned something significant from an elderly nun named Gelongma Palmo, who told the story of her younger days as an assistant to the grand lama Karmapa Rinpoche at his monastery in Sikkhim, northern India: "More than anything, I looked forward each day to my own quiet time to sit quietly on my zafu to meditate. I would get all of my chores done and, just as I would sit, someone would beckon me, saying: 'Rinpoche needs you right now.' Day after day the same thing would happen. Try as I would to just sit a little, as soon as I sat, I would be called to come. Finally, I realized I must make everything I do my meditation. And so I did.

"Right about then, a twinkle in his eye, my rinpoche (precious teacher) said that from now on, he would probably not be needing me so often—especially when I was sitting! That's how the Karmapa trained me to let go."

From a Buddhist point of view, the Dharma for daily life is encoded in the Noble Eightfold Path and what is known as its Three Liberating Trainings:

- Ethical self-discipline, which is actually a form of kindness and compassion, including social conscience, altruism, and love

- Mindful awareness in meditation and in action
- Discriminating wisdom and discernment

The Buddha's original Eightfold Path prescribes wise speech, wise action, wise livelihood, wise intention, wise effort, wise concentration, and so forth. Wisdom is obviously preeminent and essential in Buddhism, which is a wisdom tradition more than a faith or creed. Isn't it interesting that the historical Buddha, a monk, included Right Livelihood—making a life, not just a living, and finding work that grows us rather than stunts us—as one of the eight indispensable steps on the path of enlightenment? Thus, I think finding our true vocation and our true work here in this world is an important practice for lay people to enjoy, celebrate, and fully develop. We should strive wholeheartedly in our vocation, not regard work as a chore, a necessary evil, or a distraction. Very recently, at the University of Buffalo, I heard the Dalai Lama of Tibet say that we shouldn't be too ascetic or puritanical, but would do well to remember to cultivate what he called the Four Perfections: perfect nirvana; perfect happiness; the spirituality that brings us to nirvanic peace and bliss; and fourth, the temporal prosperity that provides the means for relative happiness in this fleeting life. This seems like a sensible and wise application of what Buddha called the Middle Way, a path of peace, moderation, and harmony.

We all must achieve some kind of suitable balance between need and greed. Everyone has needs, and most of us have greed; which inner creature do we want to feed? I think the Lama, when using the word prosperity, was thinking about having enough—sufficiency, if not mere subsistence—and the age-old Buddhist adage that contentment is the greatest form of wealth. I like to remember the amusing contemporary American author Tom Robbins saying, "There's a certain Buddhistic calm that comes from having money in the bank."

One of the most commonly asked questions I get in open Q & A sessions after my public lectures and workshops is how to practice Dharma (wise spirituality) in daily life. For Buddhist practitioners, the essence of Dharma in daily life is cultivating mindful awareness and discriminating wisdom on the meditation cushion. We moreover strive to carry that objective clarity and lucid, alert, moment-to-moment presence of mind into our work and play at home, the office, and everywhere in between—a reality-based mindfulness coupled with lovingkindness, active compassion, and the spirit of non-aggression.

Moreover, we need not misunderstand meditation and contemplation to be restricted only to solitude and silence, or to sitting still with eyes closed. Natural meditation often takes place spontaneously whenever we lose ourselves in the beauty of nature—a sunset, waterfall, beautiful vista, flower, garden, fireplace—or are transported beyond ourselves and into a fresh way of seeing and *being* through playing with children or pets and through music, sex, intense exercise, or dance. I've often said that connecting with nature and engaging in respectful and loving relationships are the keys to a secular spirituality today, stripped of religious dogma, partisan creeds, isms and schisms.

THE BIG QUESTIONS

Relational mindfulness, a great tool that we don't hear enough about, includes the healing power of authentically *connecting*. In essence, relational awareness means scrutinizing with conscientious attention how we actually encounter everything—moment to moment—whether from outside, inside, or in between, noticing the interrelatedness and interwoven quality of ourselves with all that lives and is. This includes how we relate to people, animals, the environment, the news, society, our bodies, emotions, feelings, thoughts, dreams, memories, desires, etc. The intentional work of conscious awareness, carried forward in every minute of every hour of every day, is the essence of integrating spirituality into daily life. It requires alert presence of mind and a heart open to all things—and is richly rewarding.

Every step of the way actually is the great Way; this is an authentic, timeless spiritual secret. Intuiting this, we enjoy *being* here while getting there. The longest journey begins with a single step, right beneath our own feet. When people ask how to integrate their spirituality into daily life, I encourage them to work with what I call the Six Building Blocks of a Spiritual Life.

1. Develop a personal, daily-ish, explicit spiritual practice

2. Study spiritual texts and reflect on their applicability to your life

3. Undertake some kind of inner-growth work

4. Find a suitable and interesting spiritual community that meets regularly, preferably weekly, and become a part of it

5. Work with experienced teachers and wise elders

6. Engage in some ongoing practical form of altruistic charitable service

Based on my Buddhist training and yoga and prayer practices, I propose these Six Building Blocks as pillars of a spiritual life that anyone can benefit from, whether or not he or she happens to subscribe to Buddhism or any formal faith. I believe that this nonsectarian, post-denominational approach expresses the essence of contemporary spirituality today and can truly change and sacralize your life. It is not necessary to practice all of the building blocks at once, or to take them up in any particular order; some may be more appropriate and doable during different stages of your life. Some may already be present in your own path and practice. All six forms of practice are tried and true methods of progressing spiritually—practical exercises that anyone can undertake and benefit from. As the Dalai Lama says, "There is no need to convert. These practices can make you a better whatever-you-are."

Six Building Blocks of a Spiritual Life

ALONE PRACTICE

I. *Personal Daily Spiritual Practice:* Personal practice is the cornerstone of a spiritual life. Practice cultivates concentration and awareness: over time, you purify and transform your illusions and delusion, thus becoming more and more transparent to innate wisdom and spontaneously expressed compassion. There are two main keys to spiritual practice. The first is to connect regularly with it: find a regular time and place; develop a regular sequence; and do it on a daily-ish basis. The second key is to find something that fits *you,* or it just ain't gonna happen! Discover which practice (or set of practices) moves and opens you, unravels you, takes you beyond yourself right into this present moment . . . and is doable within your given circumstances. Examples: meditation, yoga, tai chi, lovingkindness, chanting, prayer, connecting with nature, walking meditation. Transformative spirituality is an inside job. We all want to change the world for the better, but who is ready, willing, and able to change themselves?

II. *Spiritual Study:* Both formal and informal study can enhance and deepen your spiritual life by providing a broader context for practice. Great teachers from the past speak directly to us through the timeless writings found in every wisdom tradition. Contemporary authors and translators help us access these teachings in our own language, using modern examples. Read, listen, learn, and actively inquire: find the essential meaning of the teaching, then apply it to your attitude and intentions, explicit practice, and your life. Examples: books, journals, scriptures, myths and tales, poems. Study your life.

III. *Inner Growth Work:* As Western spiritual seekers, we are fortunate to have access to so many different skillful means. Inner growth work is an integral part of Western Dharma and can help remove inner and outer obscurations on the spiritual path. It can also help you deal with the apparent complexities of modern life: clarifying goals and aspirations, establishing priorities and setting boundaries, purifying selfishness, raising a family, making a life as well as a living, embracing a life partner, dealing with health issues, etc. Examples: self-inquiry, psychotherapy, journal writing, relationship work, creative self-expression, dietary regimes such as vegetarianism or fasting, exercise programs, healthy living.

WITH-OTHER PRACTICE

IV. *Group/Sangha Practice:* Spiritual practice within a group context provides gifts from beyond the boundaries of ego. A supportive environment enlivens practice in the good times and helps keep you on the path in the rough times. Interaction with other members will help round off your rough edges and show exactly where you are still caught by either gross or subtle forms of egotistical ignorance, attachment, and aversion. Also, you learn so much more in a group setting—others will raise issues and ask questions you didn't even know you had! Examples: church going, women's or men's circles, study groups, 12-Step recovery programs, synagogue, mosque, temple, sangha (community), retreats, pilgrimages.

V. *Teacher Practice:* Direction and guidance from a spiritual mentor or wise and experienced elder can accelerate your progress by pointing out the most direct way, helping you avoid deviations and pitfalls, and advising you through obstacles. In a very real sense, connection with an authentic teacher is no different than direct connection with the living, high-voltage current of Dharma. Ultimately, the outer teacher is the mirror in which you see your own nature reflected back at you again and again . . . allowing you to discover your best Self, your inner teacher. Examples: lama, spiritual advisor, priest, mullah, roshi, pastor, rabbi, shaman.

VI. *Service/Seva:* What is the point of a spiritual life without the intent to give back, to relieve suffering in the world, since we are all in the same boat and all rise or fall, sink or swim, together? On an outer level, cultivate action that is not just non-harming, but helpful, generous, and altruistic. On an inner level, cultivate non-ego-based intent: to serve others; to discriminate what needs to be done; to do your best, and bring forth your best inner self, no matter what. And finally, recognize that real seva, real compassion in action, doesn't have to look like anything in particular. It's essentially a quality of being, of authentic presence . . . Make a life and not just a living through engaging in one's true vocation through that naturally arising action that is effortlessly appropriate, selfless, non-harming, and full of both joy and dignity. Examples: karma yoga, compassion in action, volunteerism, right livelihood, parenting, informed citizenship, environmentalism, elder care, social activism.

I have come up with this framework after many years of teaching and observing the opportunities and challenges faced by spiritual seekers and sincere practitioners in these fast paced, post-modern times. As 21st-century Westerners, rather than medieval cloistered hermits, monks or nuns, our spiritual practice must integrate Dharma into daily life. A well-rounded spiritual life contains elements from each of these six building blocks; taking on even one of them will definitely help transform your life. As pillars of practice and a firm foundation for joyful enlightened living, the emphasis between blocks will be different for every person, according to each unique circumstances and life stage. You may choose to actively cultivate a different block each month, thus cycling through all the blocks twice a year. Or you may choose to focus on a particular block for a year or longer. Remember that continuity is the secret of success. Consistent training in all six styles of practicing over time allows you to engage fully in the world, assimilate everything into your spiritual path, and effortlessly embody wisdom in action, compassion, and impeccability. How delightful!

In the pursuit of each of these endeavors, I first encourage seekers at large to window-shop among the different spiritual and religious traditions, and then to try things on before buying them. The world's seven major religions, listed according to number of adherents, are Christianity, Islam, Hinduism, Confucianism, Buddhism, Taoism, and Judaism. Each has its own particular founders and prophets, elders, history, cosmology, scriptures, beliefs, habitual customs, manner of worship, and ways of transforming negative emotions and refining human character and emphases. The same is true for most other established spiritual paths. Being more spiritually *literate* in our close-knit, pluralistic, post-modern world can't help but open up doors of possibility in both our personal and collective spiritual lives. Just remember not to remain on the superficial level of mere dilettantism, but to eventually go deeper by actually committing yourself in one way or another. Walk the talk by actually taking up some form of regular spiritual practice.

Moreover, if we're going to examine these different paths intelligently, we need to look not only at the scriptures and the letter of their law, but also experience the spirit of it, the deeper meaning and original intent. The outer church includes the institution, the building, and the congregation of believers; the inner church is the formless yet living spirit itself; the innermost church is the ineffable mystical or direct experience of the ultimate reality underlying and suffusing it all.

Only this type of intensive investigation can do justice to our consideration of different religious or spiritual traditions. Otherwise, we're left at the mercy of mere appearances and superficial opinions, cultural and linguistic differences, and local partisan prejudices. Many people are too quick to discount organized religion as a whole simply on the basis of negative experiences or impressions they had as a child. Some are blocked by isolated points of unacceptable dogma, or scandals and disappointments involving individual religious authorities and institutions. During my own teenage years, I myself was turned off by the culture of what I'll call "suburban Judaism." I was appalled by what I considered the hypocrisy of people going to temple only on the High Holy Days and appearing more interested in proudly comparing clothes, cars, furs, jewelry, and their children's accomplishments than in objectively discussing the Palestinian issue or what the rabbi or Talmud actually had to say and might really mean. Because of my admittedly naïve and judgmental teenage perspective of Judaism back then, I never took it upon myself to look more deeply into the religion itself after completing my bar mitzvah and related studies at age 13. It was only much later, after lengthy experience with Asian religions, that I was able to more fully appreciate the profound Jewish teachings offered by, for example, the Kabbalah, holy men such as the Baal Shem Tov, and some illumined modern rabbis.

My close friend Dr. Roger Walsh has written eloquently about the universal Perennial Philosophy common to all major world religions in his insightful book, *Essential Spirituality: The 7 Central Practices to Awaken Heart and Mind*. These practices include:

- Transforming your motivation: reduce craving and find your soul's desire

- Cultivating emotional wisdom: heal your heart and learn to love

- Living ethically: feel good by doing good

- Concentrating and calming your mind

- Awakening your spiritual vision: see clearly and recognize the sacred in all things

- Cultivating spiritual intelligence: develop wisdom and understand life

- Expressing spirit in action: embrace generosity and joy of service

He describes a hierarchy of needs that demonstrates that people at different levels of understanding and stages of maturation or development adhere to and benefit from different types and depths of practices—exoteric and esoteric, personal and collective—that are preliminarily helpful and ultimately liberating.

St. Paul exhorted us to make every breath into a prayer. These profound and mysterious words are simply a prayerful version of the non-theistic contemplative practice Buddhists call constant mindfulness and alert presence of mind, in which paying total attention with every breath actually becomes both an explicit practice and a whole new way of life, unveiling the sacred dimension right before our eyes. The Old Testament says "Keep God always before you—bound to your head and your hand." This is simply another version of what I'm advocating, depending on the different forms of your own particular beliefs. It is the unwavering constancy of intention and conscious application that marks the successful integration of Dharma into every nook and cranny of daily life, infusing every single aspect of life with profound blessings, meaning, and purpose. Diligent constancy and continuous application help us progress along the path to a deeper spiritual life, whether we are pray-ers, meditators, chanters, yogis, altruists, active practitioners of non-violence, or scriptural readers. Sincerity, warmheartedness, inclusiveness, humility, and patience in our endeavors are some of the most salient secrets of success.

My late friend John Blofeld was a Buddhist author, scholar, and translator; he lived for many years in China and Tibet during the 1950s and '60s. Eventually, during the early 1970s, he settled into married life in Bangkok with his Thai wife. Once when I visited him there, John told me how difficult it was for him to get acclimated to living in such a bustling, noisy city after living for decades in Himalayan monasteries and Chinese Taoist hermitages. He said that what he found particularly challenging was practicing meditation for two hours in his Bangkok apartment each morning before leaving for his office.

In his apartment, John had created and decorated a lovely Tara (female Buddha) shrine and meditation room. The room was filled with exquisite sacred art that he had accumulated over the years—beautiful statues of Buddha; small, delicate paintings; altar pieces; Chinese brocade; sacred texts; and rare books and manuscripts, along with antique offering bowls and lamps. But despite the beauty of his surroundings, John couldn't keep the discordant sounds of Bangkok morning traffic from coming through his window and interrupting his meditation.

Then one day something "clicked" into place. It must have been a blessing from what we laughingly called "the traffic gods," combined with those from his own lineage of guides and gurus, augmented of course by the good karma he'd accumulated by faithfully persevering despite the distracting noise. For whatever reason, one morning while he was in his shrine room, meditating on Tara, he suddenly realized—Why now, and not before? he wondered—that all those honking horns, droning engines, and clashing gears didn't sound that much different from the blaring of Tibetan long horns and the crash of huge brass monastery cymbals wafting through his old hermitage window in Kalimpong, India, where John had studied Dzogchen with our late master Dudjom Rinpoche. In his master's Himalayan monastery, John had found the sounds of the horns to be an enhancement to his morning meditation. Why should the raw traffic sounds be any different now?

John told me that suddenly he realized—like awakening from a dream—that it was simply a matter of how he was perceiving those sounds—as distracting noise, or as a celestial Tibetan ritual choir—that made all the difference. Until that moment, for no real reason other than his own interpretation, he had found one set of sounds uplifting while the other brought him down.

In this way John realized for the first time the secret of the Tibetan practice of sacred outlook or pure perception—seeing all forms as transparent, rainbow-like energy; hearing all sounds as deities chanting mantras; and recognizing the Buddha light in everyone and everything. From that day on, John's morning prayers and Tara practice were totally transformed and absolutely blessed. The sacred sounds coming through his window may have been slightly different from the sounds he had heard in his guru's distant Himalayan monastery, but—in his transformed vision—they were sacred nonetheless. Thus he had found himself peacefully at home with his guru in Tara's ever-present Buddhafield, even within bustling Bangkok—a city that never sleeps.

Pure perception, or sacred outlook, is a unique Vajrayana Buddhist practice, an extraordinary means of integrating into every breath and every moment of daily life the sacredness at the heart of all and everything. In this way, through intentionally cultivating the outlook that clear light is shining through all and everything—that we are all like radiant Buddhas and Bodhisattvas, gods and goddesses, standing upon this altar of the good earth—we transform and transmute the base metal of ordinary animalistic human nature into the pure gold of the divine Buddha nature.

As Sufi poet Rumi sings, "There are a thousand ways to kneel and kiss the ground." With pure perception, every breath resonates like a prayer, every word like a blessed mantra, and every thought like a haiku—and we realize that this very land is the pure land, like nirvana, and our body is the sacred body of Buddha.

Only the snow leopards among us can go it alone. The rest of us need spiritual teachers, teachings, and friends.

—A TIBETAN SAYING

Do I Need a Spiritual Teacher or Mentor?

I have found that teachers, mentors, guides, and elders have made a huge difference in my progress along the spiritual path, as well as through life in general. The Buddha himself had two respected teachers, and I believe that Jesus also did during the mysterious "dark years". And so I say to you, with confidence, if you want wisdom in the most profound meaning of the term—study under, apprentice with, learn from, and, if possible, hang out with those who have it. Much like the native guides who helped me trek through the Himalayas during the 1970s and 1980s, wise elders function as scouts who have experiential knowledge of spiritual terrain that is far beyond our own. A masterful teacher can help us progress and develop more than most of us can even begin to imagine. This is not to say that absolutely everyone needs to find a guru; that depends on each individual. "When the student is ready, the teacher appears."

It helps to think of master-teachers as diamond-cutters, with ourselves the diamonds in the rough. Only these expert jewel cutters know where to tap along our vital flaw so that the precious stone within does not simply shatter and fall apart, but instead, opens up to reveal all its perfection. There are infinite numbers of enlightenment stories and epiphanies in the world's spiritual literature. In the Gospels, Jesus saw the tax collector Zacheus perched in a tree watching for him to walk by. Jesus called him down, and Zacheus suddenly found himself completely transformed. According to the early Buddhist scriptures, the Buddha one day spied a poor roadside flower-scavenger, Sunita, and instantly recognized his good karma and spiritual potential. Called forth to leave his wretched life behind and let his light shine out from the worldly jar in which it was trapped, as Buddha put it, Sunita swiftly became one of Buddha's illustrious and saintly disciples. There is no accounting for these transformative miracles, accomplished where individual beings encounter the powerful ripening and maturing influence of a spiritual master's profound intent to awaken and free them. More often, such profound spiritual transformation occurs after years of traditional study and rigorous practice.

Once in the 1980s, in our 3-year retreat center, my friend

asked His Holiness Dudjom Rinpoche, the head of our Nyingma School of Tibetan Buddhism: "Rinpoche, if everything is like a dream, an illusion, and not what it seems to be; how did all this mess of samsara and the world's suffering come about?" "Did it?!," Rinpoche exclaimed with a chuckle. When he said that, I personally experienced a huge shift in consciousness, a breakthrough that lasted for several hours, the ripples of which lasted for weeks and months.

Religious masters have contributed greatly to almost all the world's civilizations and have been universally admired, respected, revered, and even, at times, worshipped. The role of Spiritual Elder and Teacher, Master or Guru, is one of the most, if not *the* most, widely esteemed role and highest calling in our world, despite the fact that, as ideal types and exemplary role models, these superior individuals have sometimes been reviled, or even fallen from grace, through either politics or their own human flaws and imperfections. But how to find the right spiritual teacher, guide and master—the one most suitable for you?

In my youth, I was skeptical about authority figures in general, lumping all of them—from popes to teachers to politicians—in the same category. As a young man in college and afterwards, traveling the globe, I widely sampled the range of ideas and traditional knowledge, following Plato's dictum that the true meaning of philosophy is freedom of thought. I met many of the renowned saints and sages of that era, in both East and West. Even though I considered myself a spiritual seeker, I steadfastly refused to kowtow, bow down, submit, or surrender to the amazing gurus I encountered, or to convert or take life-long monastic vows; rather I had to be led gradually in that direction. I now recognize that rebellious period as one of transition, perhaps an essential one for certain personalities. Like an untamed, teenage bronco, I sensed a cosmic absurdity and needed to challenge any bit put into my mouth. I questioned and argued with my would-be teachers relentlessly, until I finally began to realize that their responses actually made sense and pointed to a freedom greater than merely being all by myself. They conclusively demonstrated crucial life wisdom beyond my youthful capacity to figure things out entirely alone, freeing me from constantly reinventing the wheel. Now what Aldous Huxley once called the Perennial Philosophy and the universal truths of timeless wisdom tradition lineages enter the picture.

Obviously, not everyone wants, needs, or benefits equally from having a personal mentor; people have differing personalities and persuasions, wishes, aspirations, and learning-styles. Various traditions both within and outside of Buddhism place differing emphases on the role of a teacher, but all of them stress the need for one. Catholic monks and nuns have their spiritual director, who oversees their internal development. Christian laypeople have their cleric, priest, or minister, and Jews have their rabbi. Each class of cleric has slightly different roles and relationships with congregants. Devout Hasids have their ecstatic *tzaddik* (holy man). Muslims have their mullahs and imans. Islamic Sufis have their sheiks. Native Americans have their elders and shamans. Tibetans have their lamas and rinpoches. Zen practitioners have their roshis, and martial arts students have their senseis. Hindus have a Brahmin family priest or swami and, in their later years, seek a wise saint or sage who can guide them toward higher rebirths and ultimate God-realization. A guru is called by Hindus "the doorway to God," for he or she opens the way to a higher, deeper, truer, and more timeless, deathless life. In India, ancient Hindu scriptures tell us that God, Guru, and Self are one and inseparable. This is at the heart of devotional guru yoga practice. Buddhists similarly understand that Buddha, one's spiritual teacher, and one's own true nature, or innate Buddha, are internally one.

Spiritual teachers can come in many different forms. They may be human forms, such as living masters or historical masters who function as teachers for us, like Jesus or Buddha, for example. They can be cosmic, ascendant archetypes, such as the female Buddha Tara, or the Buddha of Love and Compassion known as Avalokita or Kuan Yin. For some people angels and allies function as teachers, benefactors, guides, protectors, messengers, or prophets. Muhammad stands out as a historical tradition-founder whose guru was an angel, Gabriel. For some people, even animals can function as teachers.

Simply reading about historical teachers often raised the question for me, "How can we follow their guidance today, when they didn't face the problems we have?" I understood many of their messages to be universal and timeless; however, I wanted to find and learn from an exemplar. I wanted to know more about how these truths meshed with this life and this time. Whether these objections were true or not, the fact is that I have found that through meeting enlightened living teachers and living with elevated souls—extraordinary individuals, genuine Bodhisattvas, who embody and personify many, if not most, of the ideal spiritual qualities—something definitely rubs off. They provide exemplary models for living an enlightened spiritual life in this complex world today.

A spiritual seeker's ultimate guru is his or her own inner connection with the ultimate truth, reality itself, but external teachers reflect and embody that same truth in ways that we ourselves find it hard, if not impossible, to grasp on our own. Recognizing innate, ultimate connections with oneness can lead to accepting the need for a more formal relationship with a spiritual teacher. Sometimes these teachers may not be overtly religious people, but can still serve as spiritual guides—as mirrors who reflect back to us who and what we are along with our potential, our divine inner nature, our better angels. Parents often function in this way. So do educators, athletic coaches, music instructors, mentors, and good friends, who can serve as exemplars of selfless love and compassion, and perhaps—in the most sublime cases—as mirrors reflecting our higher selves.

Probably my first informal spiritual teacher was Professor Jon Ray Hamann, at the University at Buffalo (NY), who was my teacher and college mentor. A Dakota farm boy from a Lutheran family, he could fix anything and worked on his own car and motorcycle. He had studied theology first, then chemistry, math, and philosophy; he was also teaching at the Center for Theoretical Biology, which was doing groundbreaking research into the origins of life. I used to bring my poetry to his office so he could review it, and often joined all-night discussion, pizza, and beer sessions at his home. In many ways, I consider him to be the first teacher who really lit my spiritual lamp and inflamed my passion for truly higher learning. He inspired me to stop wasting time with things that really didn't do much for me. He taught me to live as if each day were my last, to be both curious and wondrous, to be thoughtful, incandescently alive, and to prepare myself for eternity. He convinced me that whatever I did would be magnified many times if it was done with what Buddhists call the indispensable Bodhichitta, meaning the selfless, altruistic intention to be of the utmost benefit to others. His living example demonstrated how much an integrated, unselfish, and awake individual could help others, even in small ways, like impartially greeting and wholeheartedly welcoming people. All of this inspired me to want to become more like him and to dedicate myself to something bigger than my own, narrow, self-centered, teen-age preoccupations. Jon had hundreds of students like myself engaged in accredited Independent Study under his tutelage.

Jon's example also stood me in good stead later, in India and Tibet, when it came to recognizing the value of more formal spiritual teachers who came my way. I had a sense, if only a vague, inarticulate one, of whom it would be wise for me to accept as a teacher. When people ask me today about how to find the right teacher, I want to tell them to follow their heart as I did;

but the truth is more that I followed my nose—sniffing around, checking things out, reading, questioning, discussing, and traveling many miles. The point is that we often *know* when we find the right teacher, and that intuitive knowledge comes not only from our past experiences but also from our active search for a teacher. As we go along, we become more and more sensitive to what—and who—will work for us, as well as what doesn't. It's also possible to attract the right teacher. When we intentionally prepare ourselves, work on ourselves, purify ourselves, and make ourselves the right student, the right teacher and life lessons can be attracted to us. This preparation process is not unlike consciously striving to develop and make ourselves into a more complete individual in order to find and attract a more complete and fitting mate for our personal journey of love and intimacy.

People often ask the following questions: Do I need a teacher? Why do I need a teacher? Where are the enlightened masters today? The word teacher has many meanings. It's up to us as seekers to pursue the kind of helpful expert called for by our situation, our needs and desires, and our aspirations. Experts can help with certain things, like good mechanics can fix the tricky parts of our car, although they cannot necessarily be relied upon for other kinds of advice outside their special area of expertise. Similarly, different kinds and levels of teachers can be relied on for the kind of help and expertise related to their own background and level of mastery, but not for all things under the sun. Naïve seekers and faithful devotees often make the mistake of expecting their yoga or meditation teachers to be like omniscient divinities who can guide them in every part of their life, which is extremely rare, if not impossible, today.

A body of knowledge can be taught and learned, but wisdom itself can't be taught, although it can be caught—when we catch on. Teachers impart their accumulated knowledge and experience; masters *transmit* their profound and transformative wisdom energy and blessings. Spiritual masters are like mirrors in which we can more clearly see ourselves. An enlightened teacher helps reflect our own higher potential and ultimate possibilities. A guru reflects our highest nature. As has been said, the guru, or highest spiritual teacher, is a doorway to the infinite, to the absolute, to realization, to enlightenment. We don't need to collect or overadorn those thresholds; we need to pass through them.

Various kinds and levels of teachers can help us at different stages along the path known as pilgrim's progress. There is no point in postponing your spiritual apprenticeship until the perfectly ideal Master of Masters comes along. Try to get started toward progress on the path, while keeping your eyes peeled. People occasionally tell me that they have been to India (for a few weeks) and that there "aren't many true enlightened masters alive today," but I wonder, where are the true students?

A genuine spiritual teacher or mentor is skilled, kind, selfless, reliable, patient, and generous in giving what is needed to encourage authentic transformation and spiritual emergence in his or her students, whether it's called giving birth to the Buddha, the inner Godhead, the Goddess, or the potential awakened being within each of us. A relationship with a genuine guru (Sanskrit for spiritual teacher) helps us go where we would never choose to go under the sway of our own ego, conditioning, and karmic confusion. There is an old saying in India regarding saints and gurus. The guru is a blazing bonfire—don't get too close unless you are willing to get singed, cooked, and even consumed. Even more than the general teacher-student relationship, the intense guru–disciple relationship is like a pressure cooker in which the food can cook much quicker as long as the integrity of the container remains intact.

When asked who he was, Buddha said that he was just a good spiritual friend. He later taught that the teacher is like a doctor, the student like the patient, and the Dharma teaching and practice like the medicine and the cure. The doctor can prescribe the medicine—the right teaching and appropriate practice—for the student, yet it is up to the student to take the medicine or the teaching and apply it regularly as prescribed.

For Tibetan Buddhists, the guru is considered the embodiment of Buddha himself in our lives and the source of all teachings, blessings, encouragement, protection, and inspiration. Thus a guru is said in Tibetan Buddhism to be a Buddha-like beacon in the darkness, an all-knowing master, a sighted one for the blind, a sane one among the insane, a guide for the lost, a grownup among children. An authentically masterful guru who is part of a genuine lineage of inner realization is considered absolutely necessary in order to progress on the path of enlightenment. A guru is a refuge, someone to rely on, and our guide in this life, in the bardo (intermediate passage/stage), and even in future lives. As a Buddhist teacher myself, I simply try to share my own experience and understanding with those who are interested and to continue offering support, encouragement, guidance, and instruction that can empower seekers to develop and evolve in their own genuine way, according to their deepest, truest spiritual inclination.

Spiritual teachers come in many forms besides gurus of the type I've just described. As we travel along the path, we have multiple kinds of relationships with them, with varying degrees of intensity and commitment at different times. There is no getting around the fact that, as students and learners, we each have different kinds of spiritual affinities, needs, capacities, and aspirations, not to mention personalities. We must seek a style of teaching and communicating that not only attracts us, but also inspires us toward ongoing participation, deepening commitment, and, ultimately, profound connection. It seems obvious to me that no one religion fits everyone, just as there are different courses for different horses. What's more, our personal entry point into any religion is usually a teacher or inspirational example, and no individual teacher fits everyone, just as no cuisine or style of dress fits all.

You might feel a lama or swami is your teacher. Even though he or she might not know your name, he might be your heart guru, and you might have a truly profound and genuinely meaningful relationship. I have a lot of faith in this path. Although I have a lot of faith in my teachers, I also had a lot of doubt and have always practiced what I euphemistically call healthy skepticism. I asked my teachers and gurus a lot of questions. Kalu Rinpoche used to call me "The Ocean of Questions." In the early- and mid-1970s, I lived in his Sonada Monastery in the wooded mountains outside Darjeeling, West Bengal. After his daily two-hour Dharma talk, he would ask, "Are there any questions?" He knew right where to look first in the crowd. I said one day, "Rinpoche, is it OK to ask so many questions?" He said, "Ask all your questions. Then one day you will *know*." I hope and trust that his prediction is coming true. In the meantime, I am still questioning and practicing self-inquiry, as part of my development.

A guru, as distinct from a teacher, is supposed to be an authentic spiritual master, a wise elder, a sagacious and even impeccable individual. If we are open as truth-seekers, we can learn from anyone—the wise and the foolish both—but not everyone can help guide our spiritual development in a consistently appropriate and beneficial way. Gurus are not self-proclaimed spiritual celebrities who convince others to follow them. It takes a village to raise a real master. Almost without exception, all spiritual masters and teachers exist within a lineage and tradition, are part of a community, and come from and are steeped in the learning, practices, and experiences of some school of sacred knowledge or path of conscious evolution. They too have studied, apprenticed, and learned from their masters, who learned from their own masters, and so forth. This is the meaning of authentic lineage, not merely physical ancestors and bloodlines.

Any good teacher offers encouragement and inspiration, information, knowledge, and learning, based on his or her own studies and experience. A good teacher teaches by example and shares freely with those who to come to learn and progress; but a genuine spiritual master gives of him or herself—while becoming as if part of the disciple. The venerable Vajrayana tradition instructs us to recognize the guru as Buddha in person, teaching that if we see the guru as a Buddha, we receive the blessings of Buddha, while if we see the guru as less than that, we get fewer blessings and less edification. It says that if we regard the teacher as a Bodhisattva, we receive the blessings of a Bodhisattva; if we see the teacher as ordinary, we get the blessings of an ordinary person, and we don't become as spiritually realized as an enlightened Buddha or sublime Bodhisattva. Thus the lama, as Buddha's representative or stand-in, acts as our refuge, spiritual master, guide, and protector.

We can learn from the Buddha as well, in a transpersonal way, beyond human form and contemporary embodiment as a living person. The Buddha-energy or Buddha Mind of enlightened wisdom will course through us, and eventually to others through us. We can become spiritually realized and illumined, attain transcendent wisdom and divine, Buddha-like love, and even become Buddha ourselves, as the scriptures say. It is narrow-minded to think that Buddha refers only to the historical sage of India who lived for 80 years and then passed away 2,500 years ago. The inner Buddha is enlightenment, the enlightened spiritual mind itself, which we take refuge in and rely on, and that is innate in each and all of us.

My best recommendation for finding a teacher who fits you (besides following your nose as you search around) is that only *you* should decide whom you feel most connected to, or grateful to, or whom you learn from the most. That's an inner matter. It should also be said—having stressed the importance of a teacher—that an authentic teacher selflessly strives to bring out the best in others and is there for the benefit of others, rather than for his or her own benefit. The ancient Buddhist teachings of Maitreya and Gampopa offer qualities of a good teacher for us to consider. These qualities describe one who is:

- Compassionate and unselfish in behavior

- Tamed and calm in mind

- Trained through mindfulness and meditation

- Clarified by wisdom

- Well versed in scriptures, oral transmissions, and ways of life; capable of dispelling doubts and communicating and explaining when guiding others

- Able to point out the ultimate nature of inner mind and external reality

- Joyful and generous in serving and benefiting others

- Full of lovingkindness, fearlessness, gentleness, humility, and patience

Even though a human teacher is extremely important, you should not get hung up on personality or appearance, nor be spellbound by reputation or ethnicity. Instead, focus on what they have to teach you and how you feel and *are* when you're with them or while utilizing their teachings. Buddha himself said, "Don't rely on the teacher-person, but rely on the teachings. Don't rely on the words of the teachings, but on the spirit of the words, their meaning. Don't rely on the theory but on the practical experience." If we follow this advice we won't get hung up. It isn't necessary to indulge and participate in personality cults or slavishly worship charismatic leaders. Many people think that the best teachings can be found with the most famous gurus, or that the local village guru is not as good as the head of some huge spiritual center. My experience has been that there are some very wise teachers hidden out there who are quite discreet, humble, or reclusive, or who mask their qualities.

If our teacher dies, we don't necessarily have to feel devastated, as if totally bereft of teachings and inspiration. Our teacher hearkens back to Buddha and personifies enlightenment itself, bringing to us an entire lineage of invisible allies from which we can never be parted. The Dharma (or body of teachings) is our teacher, too. The sangha (or community of practitioners) is also our teacher. John Daido Loori Roshi, abbot of Zen Mountain Monastery in Mt. Tremper, NY, has said, "Don't check out the teacher, check out the sangha. That's who you'll become." We can learn a lot from each other and from the truth of every moment. Everything can function as teacher, if we are open to it. We can learn from fools as well as the wise: how not to be, and how to be.

Finally, and maybe most importantly, we must also consider the qualities of a good student or disciple within ourselves. We must be there to learn and to grow, and be open to changing ourselves and our lives, not just to add some icing on the cake of our current life and inner being. In general, the qualities you bring as a suitable student or disciple include both willingness and ability to learn, as well as appreciation for the value of the master's treasure trove of knowledge and wisdom; honesty and openness; discriminating wisdom, freedom from prejudice or selfishness; and faithful interest, as you pursue matters devotedly, with your whole heart and mind.

In considering the qualities of a good student, Tibetan teachers often use the symbol of a cooking pot waiting to be filled with the knowledge and wisdom that nourish the spirit, suggesting that we make sure the pot or vessel is open to receiving teachings. The classic teaching, called the "Five Defects of a Pot," reminds us of essential conditions for us to be vessels for truth and wisdom:

- Being sure we are choosing the right direction (not turning away)

- Being receptive and open (not closed or covered)

- Not holding opinions and ideas that block new insights and awareness (such as being too full of our own previous knowledge, opinions and prejudices)

- Being clear, pure, and unpolluted by toxins (such as greed, pride, envy, malice, competitiveness)

- Being able to retain and integrate the teachings, making them a part of ourselves

As open vessels, we come to realize inexhaustible grace and that the ultimate blessings are wise and appropriate teachings, guidance, and inspiration. Encouraging each of us to take the responsibility for our spiritual growth and development into our own hands, the historical Buddha's last words exhort us to be lamps unto ourselves and to work out our own salvation with diligence. My own late master Lama Kalu Rinpoche taught, "You have only three things to do in this lifetime: Honor your guru. Deepen your realization of radiant emptiness, the true nature of reality. Deepen your warmhearted compassion."

11

The problem is not materialism as such. Rather it is the underlying assumption that full satisfaction can arise from gratifying the senses alone.

—THE DALAI LAMA

Can a Spiritual Life Include Sexual Passion, Meat, Drugs, and Alcohol?

HOW CAN I BALANCE SPIRITUAL ASPIRATION AND MATERIAL COMFORT?

If we are genuinely interested in leading a spiritual life and, at the same time, eager to enjoy a certain amount of worldly pleasure, then the first thing we need to work on is striking a healthy balance between these two intentions. Going toward either extreme without first realizing some degree of harmonious equilibrium between them creates instability craving, and invites failure. In Buddhism, we try to follow the Middle Way, beyond extremes. When asked about the Middle Way, the Buddha said, "It is like tuning the strings of a sitar [guitar-like instrument]. Not too tight and not too loose." I find this an excellent guiding principle. Of course, it is up to each of us to do the appropriate tuning for ourselves.

Focusing first on our natural desire for material comfort, I believe a good standard is "not too much and not too little." As a curb against excessive, uncontrolled desires, my late Thai preceptor, the Venerable Ajaan Chaa, always used to say, "Just this is enough. Just this much." It was his simplicity mantra, which I have found very helpful and load-lightening in my own life. Whenever I'm tempted to want more material comfort or sense gratification, even though I know in my heart I have enough to get by, then I just think to myself, "Whatever I have, it is sufficient; this is what's given; it's how much I get. Just this much is my exactly appropriate and perfectly lawful karmic ration, and I remain thankful for it." This is a good practice for cultivating gratitude, satisfaction, and contentment, the ultimate form of wealth.

Mahatma Gandhi said that this world has enough resources for everyone's need, but not for everyone's greed. We need to explore this relationship between need and greed, both on a personal and a collective level, in our grossly inequitable world today, where the gap between rich and poor in our own country as well as among the rich and poor nations of the world is widening dangerously. This growing gap has always, throughout history, been a precipitant for violent revolution and unrest. It is not money at the root of evil, but the overweening love of money which causes problems: greed, in a word. In this respect, Gandhi listed "seven blunders" from which arise violence in the world: wealth without work; pleasure without conscience; knowledge without character; business or commerce without morality; science without humanity; religion without sacrifice; and politics without principle. To guard against these blunders, he also listed 11 principles of "care and commitment": nonviolence, truth, non-stealing, sacred sex, non-consumerism, physical work, avoidance of bad taste, fearlessness, respect for all religions, respect for the local economy, and respect for all beings. This are wise words to live by.

There's no getting around the fact that life is complicated. It is not easy to even assess our lives in these Gandhian terms, let alone practice what we preach, walk our talk, and live the way we know we can and should. I find that it is far easier to argue about and even fight for our principles than to actually live up to them! This is one of the problems I see with much of social activism today—a gap between the doing and the being.

First of all, we have to slow down and take stock of where we are now, how we feel and why, and assess the results of the various ways we think, speak, and live. Then we can begin to determine accurate causal relationships between our thoughts, words, and actions on the one hand, and our principles, beliefs, experience, character, and karma on the other. With these insights, we can determine if we are looking for some fundamental quality in our life—for example, happiness, well-being, or meaning—and actually finding it, or if we are merely caught up in appearances, habitual instincts, and social conditioning. My lamas say that the main problem with Westerners in particular, and with worldly people in general, is that they think what they want and need is outside of themselves and that other things, people, conditions, and events are the most significant causes of their suffering or happiness, which is patently untrue. Instead, the source of our fulfillment, as well as our suffering, lies within us. An ancient, timeless Tibetan saying concisely expresses this quandary: "Worldly people are constantly pursuing happiness and generating sorrow." May we all awaken from those illusory, dream-like pursuits!

As for whether a spiritual person can also engage in acts of sexual passion, the simplest short answer is yes, of course, (unless he or she is an avowed celibate), as long as each sexual act in itself is not harmful, abusive, manipulative, or sorrow-generating. Here it could be especially helpful to reflect upon the potent tantric phrase "sacred sex," referring to the sacred dimensions of intimacy and conscious practices which help us to experience the divine in and through one's partner; as the flames of passion are transformed and transmuted into the jet fuel of compassion, human love is sublimated into divine love. Then our own loving feelings and desires are recognized as just the tip of the iceberg, and become an open gateway leading directly to infinite love.

Again the Middle Way comes into play. If we're constantly mentally preoccupied by or even addictively engaging in sex, then we're clearly straying from the Middle Way of balance and moderation. If we objectify others and see them as existing mainly for our use and gratification, then we are running away from the exquisite potential of divine love, which can be experienced through losing ourselves in another's loving embrace through unconditional loving and the union of oneness and noneness, through simultaneously uniting, dissolving, and connecting.

Oscar Wilde, a poor example of moderation but a great wit, said, "Celibacy is not hereditary." Some seem to forget, and think celibacy is required in order to pass on certain positive traits. Let me assure you that neither money nor sex is the problem, the "root of all evil"; rather, it is the deluded and incessant craving and attachment that so often arise along with them that create difficulties for us, too often becoming corrosively addictive.

In regard to alcohol, drug, or even meat consumption, the ethical challenge becomes trickier and even more a matter of personal conscience. The fact is that we're all far more likely to be consuming these things than we realize, no matter how much we may try to avoid them and the active chemical agents in them that affect our consciousness. We can't possibly avoid all chemicals, nor are we free of chemicals in our own physical makeup, but unhealthy imbalances definitely tend to wooly-headedness, soul rot, and even truth decay—spiritual conditions that become increasingly difficult to remedy.

Obviously, vegetarianism is a sensible, healthy, and compassionate option, and relevant nutritional insights and scientific knowledge abound today. However, let's not forget that even fruit and vegetable farming require the death of insects and worms, both with and without pesticide abuse, and that animals and meat byproducts, alcohol, and other drugs are "hidden" ingredients in many food, medical, and cosmetic products. The doctrine of the Middle Way urges us not to go to extremes in our avoidance of alcohol, drug, or meat consumption, but, instead, to find a balance that is suitable to our own principles, locale, chosen lifestyle, and physical, mental, and spiritual well-being. Recreational intoxicants are obviously different than meat, caffeine, sugar, nicotine, and so forth; yet to varying degrees in different people their effects can sometimes be quite similar, depending on one's individual constitution as well as frequency, intention, and context. A clear, objective, honest, and responsible conscience needs to be our guide. No one can say what is ultimately right for you as an individual, only that one is responsible for one's decisions and life. This is where developing the lucid clarity of discerning wisdom and good judgement, self-awareness, and insightful understanding becomes absolutely indispensable. Obscuring our consciousness through the unskillful use of chemical agents is not conducive to the clarity necessary to see things as they actually are and how they work, function, and are interdependent.

Many religions and spiritual traditions proscribe various kinds of foods and drugs, for various reasons and with differing degrees of severity. Even within each religion or tradition, there are various schools of thought and ways of interpreting the matter. Many Jews, for instance, don't eat shellfish or pork. Muslims traditionally don't eat pork or imbibe alcoholic beverages. Most Hindus don't eat beef. But some good people who sincerely call themselves Jews, Muslims, or Hindus don't always follow these restrictions, nor, in some cases, do their leaders. Even Mahatma Gandhi once ate fish in Calcutta, when it was presented to him. "It's what grows here," he said when queried by his close associates afterwards, who were all vegetarians like himself. On another occasion, he said that he valued truth over consistency and his life was a constant experiment with truth-finding.

In Buddhism, vegetarianism is considered virtuous, in keeping with being life-cherishing and compassionate, although it is not required as a tenet of the faith. For example, the Dalai Lama, a leading advocate of nonviolence, compassion, and environmentalism, became a vegetarian only after he escaped from frigid Himalayan Tibet, where few fruits and vegetables were cultivated, and settled in temperate India, where fruit and vegetables are bountiful. More recently, as he has entered old age, his doctors have prevailed on him to eat meat again for health reasons. Many say the historical Buddha himself ate whatever was offered to him and his followers, without particularly eschewing meat or fish. In a Buddhist scripture, the *Sutta Nipata*

245, the Buddha said, "Anger, arrogance, inflexibility, hostility, deception, envy, pride, conceit, bad company, these are impure foods, not meat." Almost needless to say, one can find other scriptural citations advocating, and even extolling, the virtues of vegetarianism. This is why one's conscience must be one's guide.

The consumption of alcohol and other drugs is generally proscribed in Buddhist scriptures; but to place this in context, the absolute proscription usually applies to ordained monks and nuns rather than ordinary laypeople. Even in the case of some monks and nuns, however—in Japan, for instance—the relevant precept says to avoid "intoxicants that cause heedlessness" or, in some texts, "substances that cloud the mind." I believe this points to the crux of the matter: whether or not we go beyond use of intoxicants to actual abuse of them. If we choose to consume such substances, we are obliged to give serious thought to how they affect our thinking, speaking, health, and actions in regard to both ourselves and others in the short and long term. In addition, after this conscientious self-scrutiny, we need to give serious effort toward limiting our consumption so that we don't over-indulge and trigger negative affects in our thinking, speaking, and living. We also need to expand the definition of drugs as widely as possible, so that we take all possible mind-clouders into consideration, including nicotine, caffeine, artificial flavorings, sugar, gambling, second-hand smoke, zoning out in front of TV, or shopping simply to make ourselves momentarily feel better.

A final thing to ask ourselves about this matter of whether or not to indulge in worldly pleasures is this: Dedication, sacrifice, renunciation, and postponing gratification are often needed in life, especially at certain critical junctures, if we are to conserve and more intentionally channel our energies in order to make room for new possibilities and latent potentialities to develop. This kind of self-restraint may not be very popular today, but it may be exactly what's required to counteract the ennui, cynicism, hollowness, inertia, scatteredness, and distractability that many of us sometimes feel—especially if we have addictive personalities. It's fine to be liberal and open-minded about how life can be lived and what we *allow* ourselves and others to do, but I believe that we need to go beyond this neutral starting-point to further the larger life we personally *aspire* to live. As we do so, we must acknowledge the value of mastering certain addictions and other unfulfilling habits, discontinuing possibly counter-productive activities, or simply training ourselves to do without what we can afford to do without. As in science, the best and most elegant solution is often the simplest. Fasting or even various kinds of abstinence can be at times an excellent and respectable option, well worth experimenting with, and conducive to conscious evolution.

I believe that today we must learn how to practice integration and balance, rather than teetotaling or puritanism. It is not that we have to get away from it all, like a hermit, or to weed out all the gritty aspects of life—sex, money, the body, relationships, emotions, conflict—to get to the real thing. The real thing, however we may conceive of it, is in any case deeper than we are, closer than we usually are to our true selves.

Riches and other acquisitions in life are not the problem, but how we hold them is. Do we have and own possessions, or do our possessions own us? The Buddha himself once advised a local king who wanted to renounce his kingdom and enter the renunciate's holy life to meditate instead on the emptiness, impermanence, and ultimately illusory nature of his jewels, palaces, pleasures, power, and prestige; to dedicate himself and all his resources to the greatest good; and to be a good steward and guardian for all his subjects, like a shepherd protecting his flock—a wise and compassionate Bodhisattva. One day that king became enlightened while meditating on the clear, scintillating diamond on his own ring. Eventually, under his enlightened leadership the entire kingdom became renowned for wisdom, peace, and harmony.

All can be the grist for the mill of our richly processing spiritual practice-path. And when it comes to finding our true path, it's what we bring to it that makes our path. We must make our karma—our fate, character, and destiny—into our Dharma, our sacred quest. We can't practice somebody else's path. That's the beauty of it. Let's strive to accomplish a profound, subtle adjustment that helps us discover that our path is right beneath our own feet, rather than looking for it afar. Just a small shift in attention allows us to turn life's ship on a dime. The path beneath our feet is not about the teacher's path or the Dalai Lama's path or the Buddha's path, but about finding your authentic spiritual path, taking responsibility for cultivating and following it, and living it fully, joyously, and incandescently.

On the Middle Way, I try to remember what I call jokingly my Zen Commandments:

- Take care, stay aware. Watch your step. Pay attention—it pays off.

- Awaken your mind, open your heart and energize yourself. Learn to see clearly and love generously.

- Find a way to live your own spiritual practice. Develop an ongoing spiritual life, not just a few spiritual experiences.

- Don't seek others' light. Exploit your own innate natural resources for a change. Mine the mind.

- Freedom is a process, not just an idea or ideal outcome. Progress is more important than perfection.

- Learn to accept, to let go, and let be. Allow.

- Lighten up while enlightening up. Cultivate joy. Don't take yourself too seriously, or it won't be much fun.

- Don't cling to anything. Recognize everything as impermanent and like a dream, a movie, a sitcom. Remember the daily mantra: This Too Shall Pass.

- Not too tight, and not too loose. Stay attuned to the big picture.

- Be mindful. Pay attention. Keep your eyes peeled. Be vigilant and intelligent about your experiments with reality.

- Be here while getting *there*, every single step of the way.

- Don't rely on mere words and concepts. Just say *maybe*.

- Don't be deceived by ideas and opinions, either others' or your own. You just can't believe whatever you think.

> *Life is precious; handle with prayer.*
> *Be good and do good.*
> *It's now or never, as always.*
> *Meditate as fast as you can.*

How Can I Remain Nonviolent in a Violent World and Deal Intelligently with Anger?

It is said that a peaceable snake who was being harassed by the village children once approached the Buddha. The snake told the Enlightened Teacher, who was well known for his gentle patience and tolerance, that the village children threw stones and beat him with sticks whenever he hunted for food. The Buddha advised the snake not to strike back and harm the children, who knew not what they were doing. Inspired by the Buddha's beatific presence and kind heart, the snake vowed to follow that sage advice. A few days later, the snake returned. Being crushed and wounded, he could hardly slither. Complaining to the Buddha, he said, "They beat me bloody, but—as you instructed—I did nothing in return. I accepted the abuse and barely escaped with my life." The Buddha replied, "Oh, poor, faithful, good-hearted snake: I did not tell you not to hiss!"

Even Mahatma Gandhi, the modern icon of nonviolence and passive resistance, admitted that using violent force might be necessary, for instance, to subdue a dangerous psychopath on the brink of seriously harming others. Gandhi taught that nonviolence must never come from weakness, but from inner strength and clarity. Only the strongest and most disciplined, principled people can hope to achieve it. This exceptional mandate is echoed in the ancient Buddhist scripture about a sea captain, a compassionate Bodhisattva, who had to push overboard a murderous pirate intent on sinking the five hundred oceangoing merchants on his ship. This story is perhaps the sole recorded incident in the entire voluminous Buddhist canon where the violent taking of life is condoned, justified as being for the greater good of the larger number—a risky rationale to put into practice by imperfect individuals or limited, partisan systems (such as our flawed American penal system).

To a Buddhist, it's disquieting to consider undertaking violent action, not to mention any sort of holy war or so-called "just" war. We all know that, usually, violence only begets more violence. At the same time, a radically nonviolent position is very hard to maintain. When I hear a senior monk and Zen master like Thich Nhat Han of Vietnam calling for radical non-violence and for intent listening, I have to ask myself, "How is it possible to listen to an aggressor bent on harming or even killing you?"

Buddhist wisdom consistently reminds us to recognize how similar, interconnected and thus interdependent we all are in this small, tenuous world. Unconditional love and warmhearted compassion are greater than ignorance and prejudice, greater than hatred, greater even than death. Twenty-five hundred years ago the Buddha himself said, "Hatred is never appeased by hatred in this world; by love alone is hatred appeased. This is an Eternal Law [*The Dhammapada*, Verse 5]." Buddhism reminds us of the fleeting, ephemeral nature of life in all its many forms. We profit by turning toward lasting values and the deeper meaning of life, thus helping instill in us a sense of the long-range view and the bigger picture.

I am quite sure that we should not immediately rush into vengeful retaliatory acts, which will only make us into the mirror image of those who have attacked us. Retaliation often brings more problems, rather than providing lasting solutions. Enlightened wisdom advocates restraint, reason, compassion, analysis, and understanding in the face of violence and aggression. Yet this should not be mistaken for mere passivity. I lived for eight years as a monk in a Tibetan Buddhist monastery, a forest cloister, under my late teacher's guidance. There I came to know how much we are all the same in what we want, need, and aspire to, regardless of how different we or our actions may look from outside, and there I learned to love even those I disagreed with and did not always like. Sacred love is greater than the dualism of mere like and dislike. That is why equanimity, or impartiality, is indispensable as one of the Four Aspects of Buddha's Love (the Four Boundless or the Four Heartitudes); for without impartiality for all, how can our loving be akin to unconditional, divine love?

One amazing discovery for me—mirrored within those blessed, peaceful, sylvan walls and contemplative gardens—was finding much of the same dissatisfaction and delusion in our monastery that exists in the world around us. All of those conflicts and illusions actually lie within us. Many noble wisdom warriors are dedicated to waging this inner struggle for equanimity for the benefit of the world, as well as for accomplishing inner peace. Being a conscientious objector amidst the collective societal madness of military warfare is a fine and principled stance, but being a spiritual activist and wisdom warrior requires even more audacity, fearlessness, and energy. As Thomas Merton, the Roman Catholic monk and spiritual activist, told us, "The rush and pressure of modern life are a form, perhaps the most common form, of innate violence. To allow oneself to be carried away by a multitude of conflicting concerns, to surrender to too many demands, to commit oneself to too many projects, to want to help everyone in everything is to succumb to violence. More than that, it is cooperation with violence. The frenzy of the activity neutralizes his work for peace. It destroys her own inner capacity for peace. It destroys the fruitfulness of his own work because it kills the root of inner wisdom which makes work fruitful."

These are subtle issues. One problem is that we don't even have a positive word for the forceful, rather revolutionary notion of nonviolence; it's sort of like being compelled to talk about non-polluting or non-littering for lack of the word ecology. A lot of people talk about nonviolence today and can readily quote past masters, from Buddha and Jesus to Gandhi, Dorothy Day, Martin Luther King, and the contemporary exemplars such as the Dalai Lama of Tibet, Thich Nhat Han of Vietnam, and Aung San Suu Kyi of Burma. But few and far between are those who actually know how to practice nonviolence on both personal and collective levels. Many purport to have ideals, but who has the accompanying courage, perseverance, intelligence, and skill to integrate those ideals into their being each day? It is often easier to fight for our principles than to live up to them.

Religion is meant to further peace, happiness, unity, and harmony, not to be a divisive force contributing to hatred, intolerance, bigotry, violence, and war. Extreme religious views bordering on fanaticism and dogmatism are forms of aggression that can lead to violence. Nonviolence is the first precept of Buddhism and a fundamental tenet of many world religions. Yet look at what actually happens in our world in the name of religion, most recently in the Middle East, Bosnia, Belfast, and

Sri Lanka. Religious extremists stir the margins of history and the shadowy borders of rogue states prone to fanaticism in order to tilt the balance towards hatred and chaos. We ourselves must not play into their hands by thinking and precipitously reacting in a similar way.

The practices of nonviolence, forgiveness, active love, ethics, and compassion are key elements of all traditional spiritual paths. This necessarily includes learning to deal with anger and hatred by purifying ourselves and rooting out anger from our hearts and minds. For over two millennia, Buddhism has stressed nonviolence, doing no harm, being helpful and altruistic, and recognizing the interdependence among oneself, others, and the entire environment. What's often not understood is the great power that underlies the possibility of the true nonviolent spirit, which can stand up to rather than being pulled down by all kinds of troubling situations and views. The power of training your own unruly heart and mind protects you from the pull to become just one more participant in the fracas.

Gandhi's *ahimsa* (nonviolence) was always coupled with *satyagraha* (truth). These two processes are practices—not just abstractions, but practical intentions we have to work at, live, and *be*. In disarming the heart, in practicing empathy, in cultivating nonviolence, or ahimsa, in ourselves, it's important to remember again and again that violence and war don't come from guns, and war doesn't entirely arise from outside of ourselves. Fyodor Dostoyevsky said that the true battlefield is the heart of mankind. We all care about, and perhaps even work for, peace in the world and in our communities and homes, and for inner peace, too, within ourselves and our relations with others. But we need to remember that these so-called "outer" and "inner" struggles are not separate; they share the same internal dynamics and resonate in the same universe. The war, violence, and aggression we see all around us is directly related to the anger, hatred, greed, fear, and ignorance in human minds—including our own. This is the root, and the only root, of these evils. It is not weapons but people who kill.

The Venerable Thich Nhat Han says, "There is a deep malaise in our society. . . . We have to look deeply together into the nature of war in our collective consciousness. The war is in our souls. Many of us are not healthy within, and yet we continue to look for things that only harm us more . . . The most important practice for preventing war is to stay in touch with what is refreshing, healing, and joyful inside us and all around us. If we practice walking mindfully, being in touch with the earth, the air, the trees, and ourselves, we can heal ourselves, and our entire society will also be healed."

Once a man had heard of the Buddha's reputation for being peaceful and nonviolent regardless of what he encountered. This man decided to test the divine one, and he traveled a long distance to be in his presence. For three days he was rude and obnoxious to the Buddha. He criticized and found fault with everything the Buddha said or did. He verbally abused the Buddha, attempting to get him to react angrily, yet the Buddha never faltered. Each time he patiently responded with love and kindness. Finally the man could take it no longer. "How could you be so peaceful and kind when all I've ever said to you was antagonistic?" The Buddha responded, "If someone offers you a gift, to whom does the gift belong?" "If someone offers you a gift of anger or hostility and you do not accept it—then it still belongs to the giver." Why choose to be upset over something that does not belong to you?

I think anger is a particularly crucial subject to talk about right now. How do we deal with that intense energy? For anger is an energy, an emotional force at first before it develops into action, perhaps in the form of violence or aggression. Energies can easily be refined, transformed, channeled, transmuted, and sublimated. When we look at anger closely and search for clues in dealing with it, we discover a whole spectrum of interrelated issues: anger itself, and then the things into which it can degenerate—hatred, aggression, violence, and rage.

Let's consider the first band of the spectrum, **anger** itself. The way to deal with anger, from the beginning, is to take the longer, deeper view, considering causes and future implications, rather than reflexively reacting. Instead of being overly reactive or unstable, or simply responding to the moment, we learn to, as it were, say to ourselves, "Count to ten," (as my Jewish grandmother used to tell me to do), thus giving ourselves a little space instead of hitting back or shouting back, or retaliating in one form or another. This provides us with the time to both find our center and to maneuver and allow our better selves, our principles, noble intentions, and mature wisdom to surface.

This helps us to create a sacred pause between a particular stimulus and our habitual knee-jerk reaction. It enables us to choose how or if to respond rather than blindly react, as we so often do—out of anger and fear, or any other negative emotion.

"When people get angry," says the Dalai Lama, "they lose all sight of peace and happiness. Even if they are good-looking when normally peaceful—their faces turn livid and ugly." One of my teachers said that when you get angry, your face shrivels up like a scorched shrimp. So you don't want to get angry! It says in the Buddha's lovingkindness teachings that if you practice lovingkindness, you'll be less angry, your face will shine, you'll be more cheerful, you'll have fewer wrinkles, live longer, and so on . . . The Buddha said, 2,500 years ago, that lovingkindness can help protect us from the destructive aspects of anger, that in fact lovingkindness is the greatest protection.

The next, more intense band on the anger spectrum is **hatred.** Anger settles in and hardens in place, spawning hatred. The antidote for this is forgiveness, tolerance, nonattachment, patient forbearance, and equanimity. We may not feel that we have these qualities naturally, but it is possible to *cultivate* and develop these positive qualities as antidotes to the poisonous ones; it is possible to actually cultivate objective clarity and to *practice* forgiveness, tolerance, equanimity, and nonattachment.

Our inner feelings of anger and hatred can degenerate even further into **aggression,** the next ring of the spectrum. (Take note that we haven't reached violence yet!) Anger is not the same as aggression and violence. We need to renounce violence and the aggression that leads to it, but not necessarily to renounce anger. Anger is an emotion. Violence is an action, one that's problematic and, inevitably, destructive. The antidote for aggression is calming our energy and quieting the mind, so that we can then be more connective—including the other, rather than seeing him or her as some alien thing outside ourselves, as an enemy that we have to fight off.

If aggression is allowed to have its way, it devolves into the fourth band of the spectrum, **violence**. For violence, the antidote is redirection and reconditioning, which happens as we rehabilitate ourselves, as we become more loving, soft, kind, generous, giving people, rather than egocentric, adversarial, selfish, mean-spirited people. We have to recognize for ourselves the harm resulting from aggressive violence and try to restrain ourselves and vow not to do it again.

The extreme fifth band in the anger-related spectrum is **rage**. What is the antidote for that? I don't know! Enlightenment, perhaps. Perhaps the antidote to the huge eruption called rage is working on the other aspects of ourselves and being more integrated and well-processed: up-to-date with our inner workings, both thoughts and feelings, so that our anger doesn't build up to that explosive pitch where we're completely enraged and out of control.

These are the five bands in the spectrum of this troublesome *klesha* (literally, defilement; also, obscuration or conflicting emotion). And the best place to get a grip is in the first band, simple anger. After much trial and error, I have come up with my own practice for regulating strong emotions and being patient and more authentically responsive. It involves five steps to Mindful Anger-management and intentional responsiveness that I call "The 5 Rs":

1. *Recognizing.* Notice with equanimity a familiar stimulus that habitually pushes your hot buttons and triggers an unfulfilling, retaliatory response—such as spontaneous harsh words. Stop for a moment to breathe, reflect, and simply relax. Actively acknowledge and feel in your body the difficult internal feelings, rather than suppressing or denying them, or ignoring the discomfort. Just being able and willing to accept that it's there can relieve some of anger's internal pressure. This definitely requires mindfulness and presence of mind—a form of conscious attention to the present moment. This continuous mindful practice can give us space for just experiencing anger as an energy, which has not yet become destructive, aggressive, or violent. Initially anger *is* just an experience, a momentary energy. Our ego hasn't yet seized on it and reacted. No violence or aggression is directed outwardly or inwardly yet. Be in the present moment—just be *with it.*

2. *Recollecting:* With remindfulness, remember the downsides and disadvantages of returning hatred with hatred, anger with anger, harm with harm. Then recollect the upsides and advantages of practicing patience, forbearance, tolerance, and stoic acceptance of karma and its repercussions. Remember the Buddhist slogan: This Too Shall Pass. In this second step, find and mine the sacred pause. Rest in it. Try to let go and let be, for a short while at least.

3. *Refraining and restraining:* Hold back your habitual negative reaction while trying to see things through the other's eyes. Cultivate feelings of genuine compassion for those who harm you, realizing that they are merely sowing the seeds of their own unhappiness and bad karma. To take it one step further, practice recognizing the adversary or critic as a teacher, a friend, and an ally in helping you develop patience and overcome unconscious, habitual, and unproductive reaction patterns. The most difficult person, situation, or illness can become our greatest teacher, our greatest opportunity.

4. *Relinquishing.* Give up habitual conditioned reactivity and let go of impulsive urges in favor of more consciously chosen, intelligent responsiveness. Accept the fact that such urges arise, rather than suppressing or indulging in them. Just feel and let them be without acting on them, and you will find that sooner or later they ultimately dissolve, especially if the habitual reaction is replaced by a different response.

5. *Reconditioning and responding.* Recall the entire situational dynamic you have now reviewed, while refraining, relinquishing, and reflecting on how little it will matter in a few months and years. Let go of unwholesome reaction patterns and intentionally choose other, more desirable ways of responding: appropriately, intelligently, consciously, and proactively, rather than reactively. This is advanced practice and can prove tricky. In some cases, it may translate into doing nothing; in others, responding with equanimity. Ultimately it means making wiser, more skillful decisions based on conscious awareness and experience. The *Tao Te Ching,* in Stephen Mitchell's wonderful rendering of it, says, "Patient with both friends and enemies, you accord with the way things are. Compassionate toward yourself, you reconcile all beings in the world."

These five mindful anger management steps are like cool, fresh breaths of mindful awareness. They can aerate a claustrophobic hour or day, help us relax and let go, and release a great deal of built-up negativity and stress amidst the tumultuous bumper-car ride of modern living. This practice can profoundly free us from falling into all kinds of regrettable reactivity, as well as the inevitably undesirable outcomes usually caused by impulsive, in-kind retaliation to anger and harm—what is usually called giving tit for tat. Let's remember that following the harsh Biblical injunction "an eye for an eye" can make us all blind.

External circumstances don't determine our karma, our character, our experience, or our destiny, but how we relate to them makes all the difference. To put it more crassly: Regardless of what cards life deals you, how you play the hand determines the game's outcome. This is the essence of inner freedom, autonomy, and self-mastery. We begin to understand the steep truth about subjectivity: that there are no unequivocally good or bad, positive or negative people, things, or events—only wanted and unwanted ones. Everything is subjective.

Holding onto anger is like grasping a hot coal with the intent of throwing it at someone else: We are the ones who get burned. The peace master Shantideva said, "Anger is the greatest sin; patience is the greatest austerity." The sixth chapter of his classic work, *The Bodhisattva Way*, is all about cultivating the virtue of *kshanti*, or patient forbearance, as a powerful antidote to anger. I consider this one of the most helpful virtues when it comes to dealing with anger and finding peace and harmony in life. The trained mind of a Bodhisattva, like a peaceful lake, is able to comfort, pacify, integrate, transform, and even transcend anger. Even if people throw sparks into it, it doesn't explode because it's like water—not volatile. The untrained mind, on the other hand, can be likened to a big pool of gasoline. Every spark makes it explode. No one can make us angry if we have no seeds of anger left inside.

Kshanti means patience and forbearance, even in the face of harm. It also includes learning to develop acceptance, openness, tolerance, flexibility and resilience, and a more broad and long-term view of things, uncoupled from temporary pleasures and pains, losses and gains, praise and criticism. In this practice, we can learn to remain centered in the eye of all such storms, which are actually only temporary weather conditions. Even emotional flux and flow are merely intermittent internal weather conditions, temporary and dreamlike. To practice patient forbearance in the face of some upset, disappointment, or irritation, simply ask yourself, "How much will this matter to me several months or years from now?"

We can work from the outside in, as well as working on ourselves from the inside out, to be better people and cultivate our noble heart. Every year 15 million people die of malnutrition. Fully one-third of the world's population is starving, according to the World Health Organization, and it is estimated that some 800 million people in the world suffer from hunger and malnutrition. Are these not manifestations of the violence and hatred wrought by greed, fear, and overweening self-interest? Are not poverty, inequality, racism, infant mortality, slavery, and illiteracy value issues we ought to be concerned about, far beyond any partisan issues or local politics?

Twenty-three hundred years ago, the Chinese philosopher Mozi taught, "To kill one man is to be guilty of a capital crime, to kill ten men is to increase the guilt tenfold, to kill a hundred men is to increase it a hundredfold. This the rulers of the earth all recognize, and yet when it comes to the greatest crime—waging war on another state—they praise it! So as to right or wrong, the rulers of the world are in confusion." The United States has been at war much of the time during the past 100 years. Today there are shooting wars raging in more than 40 countries of the world, not to mention the deadly yet amorphous war on terrorism that's being waged everywhere. If we agree that war is outmoded as a means of resolving conflict in our shrinking, yet increasingly complex, pluralistic, postmodern world, we must ask ourselves, "What shall we find to replace it?" There must be another way.

Transforming oneself transforms the world. We may not fully appreciate that paradox. It's worth reflecting on, and it's worth standing up for. Too many of the few people I know who can actually practice nonviolence long ago abandoned the political process and much of mainstream modern life. In the simplicity and purity of their own principled, simplified personal lives, they have found harmony through nonaggression—often outside of cities and the workaday world. This seems both like a loss and an untapped mine of natural resources, which gives pause for thought. It was said of Buddha and Jesus that just their presence in a village, and nothing more, would raise the consciousness of those around them; perhaps you too, like me, have experienced this when you were around highly evolved, content, aware people. They seem to radiate pheromones of love that make you feel peaceful, joyful, more at home, and secure. What would it take to bring into our busy materialistic world the experience of some of today's wise elders who live lightly on the land? Is it even desirable? Sometimes one has to get away far enough from the thing to see it clearly, and practice it clearly. The people who can talk about it don't practice it—and the people who practice it aren't participating often enough in the mainstream. The Dalai Lama himself cautions lovers of nonviolence, peace, and tolerance against what he termed misplaced forbearance, citing as an example the complacent acceptance and tolerance of things that are in fact intolerable and genuinely need to be challenged and changed.

If we want to transform the world, we must engage in it. Certainly we need to work externally for peace in the world, for disarmament among nations, and against injustice, racism, and genocide. "The gift of justice surpasses all gifts," according to Lord Buddha in the ancient *Dhammapada* (Wise Sayings). The Dalai Lama says, "I think it is important to acknowledge here that nonviolence does not mean the mere absence of violence. It is something more positive, more meaningful than that. The true expression of nonviolence is compassion, which is not a passive emotional response, but a rational stimulus to action. To experience genuine compassion is to develop a feeling of closeness to others combined with a sense of responsibility for their welfare."

When Jesus said that a victim should turn the other cheek, he was preaching pacifist nonresistance. But when he said that an enemy should be won over through the power of love, he was preaching nonviolence. Nonviolence, like violence, is a means of persuasion, a technique for political activism, a recipe for prevailing—a fearless and forceful way of speaking truth to power. We all want to change the world for the better, but who among us is ready, willing, and able to change *ourselves*, to act differently, to give up anything? This is what is needed today if we hope to see a better world, for ourselves and our descendants.

13

If you judge people, you have no time to love them.

—MOTHER TERESA

From a Spiritual Point of View, is Homosexuality Wrong?

Reverend Martin Luther King, Jr., in the face of life-threatening violence and hatred, never forgot that "all life is interrelated" and that we are all "caught in an inescapable network of mutuality, tied in a single garment of destiny. Whatever affects one directly, affects all indirectly." In expanding the vision for becoming part of and participating in the ancient concept of beloved community, King used the Greek term *agapé* to describe a universal love that "discovers the neighbor in every man it meets." This expansive love discovers the *neighbor* in every man and woman, every boy and girl: the aide who takes care of your mom at the nursing home, the woman who handles your banking, the boy who delivers your morning newspaper. When we can recognize ourselves in others, as well as others in ourselves, and realize that others, too, want, need, and deserve the same as we do—and, moreover, suffer and struggle similarly in order to achieve their heartfelt wishes and deep desires—who then can we harm? Who would we exploit? Who would we discriminate against, oppress, or abuse? If we discriminate against people of other persuasions now, who knows that it won't be our turn to be discriminated against next on the basis of our own differences of some sort or another? With this in mind, I believe that the connection between homosexuality and spirituality is more an issue of tolerance and acceptance of diversity—recognizing the dignity and human rights belonging to each of us, regardless of our sexual persuasion—rather than a specifically sexual or religious question. Thus, this currently thorny issue could well be stripped of prejudice and understood more secularly and objectively, free as much as possible of any particular religious tradition's overlay.

Most straight people who have known and admired gay people come to realize that gayness is a fundamental and inseparable component of what makes gay people who they are. Right now, right here at home, some of my students, friends, and colleagues are gay. My first yoga teacher long ago in India was gay, and many of my favorite writers are (or, in the case of deceased writers, were) gay. The most helpful clerk at my favorite local deli is gay, and some of my meditation center's board members are gay. A young schoolteacher I knew was gay—until he committed suicide because he was unable to find his way out of the closet. From my experience with these gay people and others, I can speak confidently about their right to full membership in society. The American Psychological Association (APA) recognizes that sexual orientation is most often not a choice at all, but the result of a complex interaction of environmental, cognitive, and biological factors. Even more significantly, the APA clearly states that homosexuality is not an illness and, therefore, not in need of a cure.

As far as Buddhism is concerned, the evidence seems to suggest that Buddhism has been for the most part neutral on the question of homosexuality. The Buddha himself, like Jesus, said nothing about homosexuality, as far as modern scholars can tell. Over the centuries, since the time these religious leaders taught, various spiritual traditions and scriptural commentaries arose in different societies and eras, each of which typically regarded homosexuality in terms of the prevailing cultural mores and beliefs. For the most part, however, homosexuality was a matter that was considered so outside the pale of "normal" living that it was given little attention—and, when it was, it tended simply to be dismissed in a blanket condemnation. Perhaps it is useful to keep in mind that the term homosexuality is a 19th-century

European invention, and the notion of a homosexual lifestyle didn't really exist before then. I like to remember what Nietzsche once said about definition: "Anything that has a history has no definition."

Like definitions, quotations are also elusive; a quote by definition is out of context. Be that as it may, the Dalai Lama once said, "It is wrong for society to reject people on the basis of their sexual orientation. . . . There is no harm in mutually agreeable sexual acts . . . In the context of time, culture and society . . . if homosexuality is part of accepted norms, it is possible that it would be acceptable." Yet he is less permissive and tolerant about homosexual conduct in regard to Buddhist practitioners as opposed to members of society in general. Another time he said practitioners in the West need to figure this issue out for themselves. When the notable Buddhist abbess Mindroling Khandro Rinpoche of India was asked about gay love by Buddhist practitioners during her visit to San Francisco in 1994, she said, "Homosexuality is nothing different, nothing new. It was there a long time ago in Tibet, in the East, in the West, everywhere. . . . If you really love another man as a man, no problem. One can grow spiritually through homosexual relations." This is obviously not a view that everyone within or outside our tradition necessarily agrees with, although I do.

Why do we single out homosexuality as a religious issue when most world religions generally frown on sexuality and passion in general? The principle question for Buddhism throughout the millennia has not been homosexuality versus heterosexuality, but rather sexuality versus celibacy, and committed sexual relations versus polygamy and promiscuity, or even abusive, nonconsensual or addictive behaviors. The historical Buddha did proscribe sexual misconduct, which he defined simply as anything that is harmful to others or to oneself. He also considered that, for serious spiritual aspirants, any behavior not conducive to the realization of enlightenment is misconduct, whether sexual or another aspect of worldly activity. The fact that originally Buddhism seems to have been essentially neutral in regard to homosexuality does not imply that the cultures in which Buddhism arose and later flourished have always been neutral or flexible. Some have condemned or at least demeaned it. Others, at times, have been tolerant of same-sex relations. Certain strands of spiritual tradition and practice—tantra (the mystic tradition in Buddhism), for example, and some of the world's Goddess-related sects—have been and continue to be interested in integrating passion and sexuality into the sacred path of transformation and spiritual realization, unifying the mind/body split through sacramental sex. For many centuries tantric practices, which lead to the transformation and sublimation of passion into compassion and translate the animalistic side of human nature into the sublime side of our divine or Buddha nature, have provided a viable path of awakening for those capable of benefiting from such powerful and profound, non-dualistic teachings—integrative practices that exclude no aspect of life or of human nature from the spiritual domain.

Both Buddha and Jesus taught about love and compassion, the dignity and miraculous nature of life and of individuals, the marvel of humanity and its inner good-heartedness, and the need to empathize with the marginalized, the oppressed, the child, the poor, the underdog. Moreover, both seminal teachers exemplified penetrating wisdom and straightforward actions that cut through hypocrisy and such prejudices as caste and class privilege, gender inequality, and racism. Both Buddha and Jesus, as master teachers, saintly individuals and religious founders, fundamentally knew suffering and the way out of suffering to bliss and peace. One of my colleagues told me that he came to Buddhism through his suffering—the suffering he faced in the process of fully accepting his homosexuality. He said that he did not hide himself in the practice of meditation, which is often viewed by non-Buddhists as the main practice of Buddhism. Instead, he nurtured himself in the Buddha's understanding of suffering, the causes of suffering, and the way out of suffering through the Eightfold Path of enlightenment. The Buddha and Jesus exemplified for us the highest living examples of unconditional love and impartial compassion for those who are suffering, confused, lost, excluded, or downtrodden. The Buddha teaches us that suffering comes from attachment, aversion, and delusion—delusions that arise from a false view of self; that is, a solid little egoic self that is separate and functioning alone, independent of the whole of humanity.

Being lesbian, gay, or bisexual is simply the way that some people are created. Yet because lesbians and gays constitute a minority in our culture, they are inevitably subject to prejudicial treatment, not to mention prey to misunderstanding, fear, doubt, mistrust, and marginalization. The only practical human way that I see to resolve such a dilemma is for straights, gays, and lesbians to focus more on what they have in common with the majority and continually strive to build an understanding of each other from there. Unfortunately, too many straight Americans seem determined to notice only the differences between them and their lesbian and gay compatriots and overlook the many similarities and interdependences that all share.

I have noticed that difference is a curious thing. When we focus on difference as a central lens for judgment, we limit our potential for bringing our own full selves to the world. When we look through a straw and focus solely on that narrowed view of reality, we limit both clarity and wisdom, as well as constrict our potential for living an awakened and loving life. Doesn't any objective human perspective preclude mistaking one part or characteristic of a person or peoples for the whole? Have we learned nothing about the injustice of regulating such activities as hiring, remuneration, school admissions, and voting, sitting on a bus and drinking from a water fountain, according to a single strand of a person's being, such as color, gender, nationality, or religious persuasion? This reminds me of the Buddha's saying that most of our opinions resemble those of the blind men who defined an entire elephant as either a rope, a hose, a pointed pole, a rough, hairy wall, or a pillar, depending on which part of the huge creature each was feeling: tail, trunk, tusk, side, or leg.

Unfortunately many of those without eyes to perceive unity amidst diversity and see the significant underlying patterns, as well as individual pieces, are karmically predetermined to notice only difference. In addition, too many people indulge in invoking their own particular religious prophets as universal arbiters of conscience in this rather intimate and personal matter. They even seek to institutionalize a permanent difference by refusing to let gays share the civil right to marry. My colleague, who has participated in numerous panels on the topic of homosexuality, said he would often come up against Christians for whom this topic is theoretical (or so they think), simply because the issue hasn't come to life in their own personal world. Research has found that the people who have the most positive attitudes toward gay men and women are those who say they know at least one gay, lesbian, or bisexual. For this reason many psychologists today believe that prejudices toward homosexuals are not grounded in actual experience, but rather on stereotypes and misinformation.

Both Jesus and the Buddha devoted their lives to promoting tolerance, acceptance, and inclusiveness, while avidly protecting the outcast. If they were alive today, I'm sure they'd assume a similarly radical activist role and identity as social reformers. I think we can all guess in our heart of hearts how they would feel about denying a person civil rights (such as marriage) because of whom he or she loves. Drawing a parallel between the gay-lesbian campaign for equal treatment under the law and the ongoing African-American civil rights movement, Coretta Scott King, widow of Martin Luther King, Jr., noted, "What we see in both situations is a tyranny of privilege, an unjustified, selfish desire of the haves to keep others from having." I agree with her, and I also think there is a great deal of fear, prejudice, intolerance, and ignorance at work in these social injustices.

Robert F. Kennedy, delivering an impromptu eulogy for Dr. Martin Luther King, Jr., from the back of a flatbed truck during a campaign stop in racially charged Indianapolis, Indiana, stated, "What we need in the United States is not hatred, not violence or lawlessness; but love and wisdom, and compassion toward one another, and a feeling of justice toward those who still suffer within our country, whether black or white." I believe that in future centuries, many, if not most, of our ancestors will look back with both incredulity and horror at the abuse people have endured in our times due to the politics of sexual orientation. I believe they will recognize this particular form of discrimination as not unlike the racism and sexism of previous eras.

Do we realize how often the fears, doubts, and insecurities within us condition us to need an outside enemy to reinforce and stabilize our false notions of ourselves, both individually and collectively? This drives us to divide the world into "us and them" so we can more easily discriminate, keep score, and identify who is right and wrong, good and bad. We seem to want a world that imitates the classic cowboy movies, where the good and bad guys are clearly delineated by their respective white and black hats. This sort of simplistic moralism may be fine and fun when it comes to rooting for one's home teams on the sports fields, but is far from amusing and quite counterproductive when it spawns the horrors of slavery, racism, homophobia, xenophobia, and genocide. Even religion, which is by definition supposed to be a uniting and harmonizing force, has apparently become an aggressively divisive force in our violent world today through one-way extreme views and dogmatic beliefs.

In recent years, whether or not to grant homosexuals the same rights as straight people, including the right to marry, has remained a hot-button issue on the American political scene. I live in Massachusetts, which at the time of this writing is the only state where homosexual marriage is legal. However, it has not always been tolerant, open-minded, or accepting of diverse views and beliefs. Almost 400 years ago, the pioneering English Puritans who landed on this shore—themselves seekers of religious freedom—were fundamentalists who drove out people who didn't adhere to their strict Calvinist interpretations of scripture, including religious leaders like Roger Williams and Anne Hutchinson. In a similar vein, much of the current opposition to same-sex marriage in America has been fueled by people who condemn homosexuality on religious grounds.

Discrimination and prejudice are not happy parts of our human heritage. For example, it has taken much too long to eradicate racism in America, a problem that still persists among us. In my opinion, same-sex marriage should be acknowledged everywhere as a civil right. I do not see it posing any threat to, or interference with, the sanctity of traditional marriage. Over 30 years ago, in 1975, the American Psychological Association adopted a policy statement regarding homosexuals that includes this statement: "The APA deplores all public and private discrimination in such areas as employment, housing, public accommodation, and licensing against those who engage in homosexual activities . . . Further APA supports and urges the enactment of civil rights legislation at all levels that would offer citizens who engage in acts of homosexuality the same protections now guaranteed to others on the basis of race, creed, color, etc."

Almost each and every culture throughout history has had its own interpretation regarding mores, encoded variously as laws or as acceptable customs and manners. It bothers me, however, that in our allegedly democratic nation, where church and state are supposedly separated, one particular religious persuasion, laying claim to universal values, can be allowed to influence public debate and legislation in such a strong, partisan manner. I refer specifically to the Christian fundamentalist opposition to same-sex marriage, openly expressed in political contexts. I personally believe same-sex marriage is a matter of civil rights, which exist apart from individual religious sanctions and prohibitions and do not depend on majority rule.

In February 2004, Mayor Gavin of San Francisco instituted his own social reform by ordering the city to provide civil marriage licenses to all applications without discrimination according to sexual orientation. Watching the events unfold, I was heartened by the joy and love that the newly married same-sex couples showed to each other and to the world. It was a transforming experience for me and many of my Buddhist friends and colleagues to see such happiness and to appreciate the rightness of it. Gay clerics of various faiths spoke out, often for the first time, about their sexual orientation vis-à-vis the teachings of their own churches. Would it be too much to disclose that some of the most exemplary leading religious and spiritual teachers I know today happen to be gay?

I agree with the writer and public commentator Jon Olsen, who said in a recent editorial in the *Minneapolis Star Tribune*, "Let the churches that reject gay marriage do so—and determine their own course. But stay out of our legislatures and courthouses on this point. . . . The churches will survive, and the marriages they bless will survive, whether or not gays marry. Can the state survive if it practices discrimination so deliberately? To abandon the principle of equal justice under law—to write law to specifically exclude a class of persons from entering into a marriage agreement—chops away at America's roots. Doing so at the behest of the religious class kills a part of its soul."

One of my students, a university professor, told me about recently showing a video in her class that raised civil rights issues. After witnessing views that were not identical to the ones he learned as a child, a class member said, "Well, what am I *supposed* to think?" It's a good question, because it's clear and honest and the best type of beginning for a deeper quest into the truth of the matter. What *are* we to think? As the Buddha taught, if you genuinely wish for certainty, you must find it for yourself, for deep conviction cannot be given to you by anyone else or by any doctrine. It cannot simply be imposed on you, with the expectation that it will be absorbed and become part of you, without any questioning, testing, or actual experience to further reinforce and integrate it into yourself. Doesn't the egotistical "us and them" mentality lead directly to judgment, separation, fear, and insecurity and away from meaningful connection, empathy, and compassion? Novelist Alice Walker writes, "I think that we have to own the fears that we have of each other and then in some practical way, some daily way, figure out how to see people differently than the way we were brought up to."

So how can we individually and collectively see this question from higher ground? These words from UNESCO (The United Nations Economic, Social, and Cultural Organization) on the subject of tolerance may be instructive: "Tolerance is respect, acceptance and appreciation of the rich diversity of our world's cultures, our forms of expression and ways of being human. Tolerance is harmony in difference. It is not only a moral duty; it is also a political and legal requirement. Tolerance, the virtue that makes peace possible, contributes to the replacement of the culture of war by a culture of peace."

Unfortunately homosexuals are at a higher risk for physical assault and violence than are heterosexuals. In one study of 500 gay young adults in California, half of them admitted to having been a victim of some form of anti-gay aggression, ranging from name-calling to physical violence. To correct this situation, we need to cultivate greater tolerance among the members of society at large. I like the following definition of tolerance, which helps steer Teaching Tolerance, an organization of educators founded by Morris Dees of the Southern Poverty Law Center: "Tolerance is not a concession, condescension or indulgence. Tolerance is above all, an active attitude prompted by recognition of the universal human rights and fundamental freedoms of others. In no circumstance can it be used to justify infringements of these fundamental values. Tolerance is to be exercised by individuals, groups and States. It means accepting the fact that human beings, naturally diverse in their appearance, situation, speech, behavior and values, have the right to live in peace and to be as they are."

Until we can each experience the genuine compassion that comes from knowing what it is to be "different" and until we come to know the interdependent web that is the true nature of reality, where does tendency toward divisiveness end? I have had my own little prejudices; for example, against Germans, due to the biases I inherited from my Jewish relatives who lived through the Holocaust era. My father would never buy a Volkswagen or visit Germany as a tourist, although he and my mother traveled a lot internationally over the years. I never really understood prejudice and discrimination from the inside, however, until I was discriminated against myself. Perhaps empathy, identifying with the victim, is the way to undo the yawning chasm between us and them—a chasm which keeps us feeling separate and apart, and prevents us from feeling what they feel, knowing where they are actually coming from, and thus coming closer to the possibility of mutual understanding and genuine tolerance. Perhaps through such a shift, we come to see through the illusion of separateness and begin to see more deeply into King's view of beloved community.

When we come to perceive our interconnectedness, we come to know that fundamentally we each want and need the same things—we each want happiness and we don't want suffering. Then we begin to see through the veil of illusion that obscures our views to the point where we wind up justifying or even passively accepting the denial of civil rights. A true awakening would have us step back and expand our awareness that *all* living beings are impacted by our thoughts, speech, and actions. If we can develop this awareness, we naturally come to universal love and compassion for the welfare of all "others." We might even notice someone amidst our daily routine standing a little taller and straighter, and breathing more freely.

14

Life's most persistent and urgent question is: What are you doing for others?

—DR. MARTIN LUTHER KING, JR.

How Can I Balance Taking Care of Myself with Helping Others?

Life asks a lot of each of us. How we respond to life's demands and mysteries makes all the difference. How healthy is our relationship to giving and to receiving? How generous—or for that matter tight-fisted—are we in sharing our material resources, as well as our talents, abilities, personal time, and energy? This is an election year, but every year is and every day is— and every moment, in one way or another. We are constantly "voting" with our words, thoughts, and deeds for how the world is and shall be.

In life, as in bicycling, balance is everything. No one needs or benefits from a weary, burnt out, victimized, co-dependent helper, social activist, volunteer, or overwhelmed martyr. Yet each of us must do what we can, as we can, when we can. Balance is found not in trying to control others or in trying to manipulate outcomes, but in living fully in the moment, while being present for others without unrealistic expectations or selfish demands. Such goodwill and generosity—giving ourselves to every moment through lucid *presence*—can sustain an inconceivably delicious lightness of being. As the Buddhist master Atisha said, "Always maintain a joyous and open mind." Buddhist wisdom, like Jesus' essential message, instructs us to put others before ourselves. In fact, the first virtue on the 10-step Bodhisattva Path is self-giving generosity. The Dalai Lama himself has said that the distilled essence of Buddhism is, in a nutshell, altruism and warmhearted kindness. So: How to balance one's legitimate needs with those of others?

The universe has put someone in charge of you—none other than *yourself*. The law of karma is utterly aligned with this reality: We alone are principally responsible for our experience and our life, and for living in congruence with one's true Self. Rabbi Hillel, the ancient Jewish teacher, said, "If I am not for myself, who is for me? But if I am for my own self only, what am I? If not you, who? And if not now, when?" No single one of us can do it all or is in total control, yet none are exempt from participating. This precept clearly points to a genuine middle way, beyond the extremes of self-denigration and low self-esteem on the one hand and solipsistic selfishness and egocentric narcissism on the other.

When faced with difficult judgments and decisions, I like to ask myself, "What would unconditional love call forth in this situation? How much shall I give? How much *can* I give? What is enough, what is right, what can I do?" These are important questions we have to answer, in many little ways, every day of our lives. Should we give money to every beggar we pass? Speaking personally, I don't think so, despite how beautiful that practice may be for someone who can genuinely afford the time and money involved. We must each give what we can, when we can, and always give of ourselves, without habitually tending toward so-called ratio strain, where too much is going one way rather than the other(s). My friend Joe Gleissner, a Roman Catholic Good Samaritan who has dedicated his entire life to the poor through affordable housing projects, advises not to give change to panhandlers, but instead to donate to reliable charitable organizations where the money will be put to good use. I myself try, as a spiritual practice, to give *something* to everyone who asks—if not money, at least a smile, nod, or "God bless you" in passing. A Bodhisattva learns through training as well as trial and error that every encounter—however brief, superficial, positive, or negative—can be meaningful, can be beneficial. It depends on how you relate to it, and your intention, too. No one way fits every occasion.

It's important to keep in mind that we have to be able to receive as well as to give. Some people focus mainly on the giving, and thus tend to overextend and burn themselves out. They may even, for their own unconscious reasons, hijack all the giving in a relationship. In doing so, they undermine the chances for true reciprocity and mutuality in that relationship. We hear a lot in Buddhism about altruism and unselfishness, but this doesn't mean getting totally out of balance and entering into self-denial and ascetic deprivation. The reason that so many religious scriptures and secular humanitarian value systems emphasize giving to others is that most of us are immaturely inclined toward the opposite extreme—greed, egotistical self-involvement, self-indulgence, selfishness, and self-reinforcement. The Middle Way bids us to be as open to genuinely receiving as we are to giving—like breathing in and breathing out. Every moment we are sharing in and co-mingling with our world, beyond the need to force or resist. Everything flows, changes, and morphs into something else. We cannot hold or stop this river of life—at least not for very long.

The beauty of authentic, spiritually based, voluntary simplicity as a practice lies in trustfully surrendering ourselves to a higher power and purpose, avoiding self-destructiveness or low self-esteem. Losing one's self in the wrong way is what Tibetan Buddhists call "turning the god into a demon." Some examples of the demon include: claiming our good deeds as justification for feeling superior to or overly judgmental about others (holier than thou); resorting to benevolent acts of charity and workaholic-like busyness as means of avoiding intimacy problems with our own loved ones; or volunteering simply out of fear of meaningless solitude and boredom. We also lose ourselves when we fall into the codependent trap of immature boundaries—not knowing where self ends and other begins, and losing touch with our own authenticity. This includes the disease to please, in which we compromise our own needs, preferences, and principles by compulsively shaping and adapting ourselves to others' perceived wants and needs, desires and demands. It also includes the need to be needed in order to feel indispensable and secure from abandonment. It is often helpful to reflect on what we are truly responsible for versus what we merely feel obliged to do out of some vague sort of compulsion or complex. Responsibility is above the cutoff line and needs to be fulfilled; obligation is often below the cutoff line and needs to be questioned, as in the "I had to say yes to her request to drive me to the airport." We do well to reflect upon who and what fuels an inner sense of obligation and try to gain more clarity about our choices.

Think about the people you have a hard time saying no to, and why, and what the downsides might be. Reflect upon the state of health of your own boundaries. Ask yourself if you are perhaps suffering from the disease to please. The Buddhist practice of cultivating compassionate, impartial equanimity includes calling to mind this phrase, to balance our feelings of obligation, codependence, and enmeshment: "Everyone is responsible for their own experience; their happiness and sadness does not fundamentally depend upon me." And yet the activist and Bodhisattva in the world, the Dalai Lama of Tibet, reminds us: "We need each other in order to become enlightened. We need others to genuinely develop and realize compassion, without which the realization of wisdom and unconditional love is not possible."

I once heard a woman remark to a visiting lama from Nepal, "I want to help others, but there's so much more that can be done, and sometimes I just get tired and don't have the energy. It seems like there's no end to the suffering and injustice in this world. What should I do?" The lama advised this young, would-be Bodhisattva that whenever she experienced weary aversion toward doing something she thought worthwhile, she should take a reflection break to allow the momentum of events pulling her forward to settle, and to rejuvenate and restore herself before re-applying herself to the task at hand. Finding compassion and inner clarity for herself, it seemed, was the essential first step she needed to take if she were going to have the resources to serve others wholeheartedly and in a considered, healthy manner. This message conveys the interconnectedness of us all and the need for each of us to take care of ourselves, as well as others.

The ideal, of course, is that our life as a whole becomes our service and contribution, a coherent mission, rather than any particular set of individual acts (such as giving money to every beggar). My friend's grandmother, Alice Mae, claimed clergyman Edward Everett Hale's bracing words as a life-motto of service: "I am only one, but I am one; I cannot do everything, but I can do something. What I can do, I ought to do; and what I ought to do, by the grace of God, I will do." She was overheard in her room praying aloud at the age of 102, "Dear God, just tell me what you want me to do."

Altruistic service is like the tax we gladly pay to contribute to a better world and a more beautiful life. Alice Mae lived a life of selfless service, offering herself entirely up to her world, while having the wisdom to know to the middle way, to live according to a balance that sustains. I try to use Buddha's wisdom eye within my own heart and mind for discerning balance questions. I don't "see" with this eye what Buddha himself would do, but, rather, what *I* could do, according to my highest and inmost wisdom, which is my own innate Buddha-nature. This helps me decide the wisest, most compassionate, and most appropriate all-around action (or non-action) to undertake in each situation. It helps me to align with a higher purpose, a more central, vital organizing principle than my own merely ego-based needs and desires. It helps free me from mistaking action and movement for *meaning*.

Don't we all have within us, in our higher conscience or consciousness, an inner guide to help us make mature decisions, combining the wisdom of the past, the insights and perceptivity of trustworthy people around us, and our own sense of the truth of things? Isn't it right to follow this guide as our conscience, rather than a strict formula or recipe, in our acts of generosity? Our guide can help us learn how to find the balance between caring for ourselves and for others, between stirring up the inner wellspring and offering it to others. Once we've found this balance, the wellspring will get broader and wider and more productive, creating what poet May Sarton calls "the gentle revolution" that "springs from the imperative need to bring imagination, tenderness, and human compassion to bear in regions where they have often been denied access."

As we learn to find the wisdom to sustain this balance, we move on to the next, more subtle question: When do we intervene in a situation that looks troubling to us? What if we know that a good friend's husband is cheating on her—do we tell her? What do we do, if anything, when we realize someone we love is destroying himself by abusing alcohol or drugs? Mistreating a child? Shutting out the world? Deluding him- or herself? Above all else, we must be compassionate, patient, and caring toward those who are going through rough times. The Dalai Lama tells us, "Sometimes we misunderstand compassion as being nothing more than a feeling of pity. Compassion is much, much more. It embraces not only a feeling of closeness, but also a sense of responsibility. So compassion and love, embodied in an attitude of altruism, are qualities that are of tremendous importance for the individual, as well as for society and the community at large." But does our supposed clarity and compassion give us the right to confront others or take steps toward alleviating their situation when they haven't given us any invitation or opening to do so? (Needless to say, the ground rules are slightly different in the case of minors for whom we are responsible and in other situations of explicit guardianship.)

When we begin to consider intervening in someone's life, it is important to remember the following six matters:

First, *reflect upon ways of connecting.* It is simplistic to think that our only recourse in such a situation is a deliberate, forceful action with a specific agenda and a clearly anticipated outcome: the classic intervention. Much of life unfolds below the radar in the gray (ambiguous) areas, without the need for dramatic gestures. People interconnect with and mutually influence each other, for better or worse, all the time in many different ways: verbally, nonverbally, physically, intellectually, emotionally, energetically, psychically, spiritually, and socially. In light of secret, private knowledge of some trouble a particular person is facing, we can possibly take the initiative to work creatively and compassionately on some of these levels to help make a difference. Perhaps as a result, the person will more easily and productively come to the point where he or she can open up and confide in us. Maybe we can even influence the person to make positive changes or uncover the truth on his or her own, without the need for any intense conversation or overt physical intervention.

Second, *check our intentions*. Are our generosity and caring authentic, or do we have hidden, mixed motives? We must ask ourselves, "Why is it that I want to intervene? Am I doing this for them or for me? Is it out of love and compassion, or is it out of pity, anger, self-righteousness, compulsion, or perhaps the need to feel better about myself? Am I meeting this person where he or she truly is, or am I coming to this person as a superior, or in the holier-than-thou mode, my message filled with 'you shoulds' and 'if only you woulds'? Am I sure I am not jumping to conclusions? What might possibly happen when I intervene? How can I most compassionately handle each possibility? What would Buddha do here? What would wise King Solomon do?"

If someone is drowning, it is noble and natural to want to jump in to save this person. But shouldn't we first consider whether we *can* save them? Can we swim? What are the water conditions? If we can't swim, is it right to sacrifice our own life to less-than-realistic possibilities for helping? Impulsive actions, however noble-seeming, may not always be the most appropriate and effective. In the Mahayana Buddhist tradition, the action of the Bodhisattva—the awakened wisdom warrior working for the benefit of all—soars upon the wings of both wisdom and compassionate, skillful means. The latter requires not just seeing what to do and knowing what is needed, but knowing how to do it in order to accomplish the best outcome. Many a compulsive do-gooder has tried to help out and just stirred up the dust, to everyone's detriment.

Third, *remember that listening is often the greatest help we can give someone.* Listening at its core involves simply being present for the other individual, without judgment, without distancing, and, most of all, without the "you shoulds," "why don't yous," and "the way I did its." The latter are easy, fast, knee-jerk types of superhero interventionist comments, which seldom prove effective and are often resented. In many cases, the greatest intervention is just being there, living into the grace of the moment with the other person. Lending an ear, a non-judgmental accepting presence, or a shoulder to cry on may be greater gifts than we realize. Let's not overlook the interactive, interwoven, and meaningfully interconnected nature of real relationships when we practice Just Listening, and remember to do it actively, dynamically, warmly, and empathically (even if sometimes silently). Responsive, dispassionate listening is a therapeutic art and a vital form of giving and loving, which can lead to, and further promote, intimacy and understanding, healing, and spiritual development.

I remember meeting with one of my students, a brilliant young man who had earned a master's degree in physics from the Massachusetts Institute of Technology. He suffered from severe depression and suicidal thoughts. I intentionally intervened in a small way, when I e-mailed him to see if he was all right after he had missed class for two weeks. It's something I don't often do with students, but I felt an intuition about his plight. As it turned out, he had slipped into a deep depression, had been to the hospital, was under the care of a psychiatrist, and was doing everything medically he was supposed to be doing. I remember sitting with him a few days later and knowing there was not much more I could do other than pray and be silent, cradling him in my heart and meditations, for the greatest gift I could give him would be to completely accept him where he was and encourage and support him by holding him in spirit through the inner warmth of caring, love, and compassion. I just listened and listened and listened. Months later he told me how therapeutic it was to talk with me, for I was "someone who really understood him, at last." (Remember that I had only listened to him.) Think of that word, understand, or "standing under." Simple, silent, but intentional support and subtle encouragement is sometimes the only thing necessary to achieve a breakthrough.

Fourth, *keep an open mind*. We must always bear in mind that we probably don't have the full picture. Isn't it possible that we might not know all the facts about the situation we face, and that if we were more fully cognizant, we'd have a different opinion? When we have a flexible attitude and open mind, problems do not seem insurmountable, but when our minds are small or closed, each problem seems huge, complex, overwhelming. Knowing the balance between skillful action and appropriate non-action is tricky and requires discernment, as well as patience and timing. Being nonjudgmental, tolerant, and accepting is fine, up to a point; however, objective discriminating wisdom is adept at making judgments, choices, and decisions as needed. This is where a practice of serene inner stillness is important. Learn to be able to remain centered amidst the storm and to listen to your own inner teacher, the voice that can guide you each and every moment. Singer-songwriter Meredith Monk once said, "That inner voice has both gentleness and clarity. So to get to authenticity, you really keep going down to the bone, to the honesty, and the inevitability of something."

Fifth, *recognize that good friends, teachers, and benefactors tend to point the way rather than take command of the journey*. They don't try to tell us exactly what to do, or to change us in their desired way; rather, they model, reflect, facilitate, listen, care, provide a sounding board, and ask questions. Research reveals that people don't really change until they are ready to do so, are so motivated, or are forced to do so through inner desperation and a lack of options. We can't do the changing for them. We would do well to remember that, or at least to consider it, before leaping into any intervention. One secret to relationships is learning *with* rather than *from,* or trying to instruct or change the other. If you want a deeper secret teaching about relationships, here it is: There is no separate other.

Sixth, *safeguard against attaching to particular results and short-term, immediate outcomes.* Since we rarely if ever see the full cosmic picture, we can't predict what may or may not happen as a result of our efforts. But we can trust in this: If our intentions are pure and we are acting out of authentic love and compassion, and we utilize skillful means, our noble efforts are like sincere offerings, bound to have beneficial results, even if we may never see or know about them all. So once we've done what we can, we need to let be and let go. We must not conduct a constant accountability check. As Lao Tzu said in his classic text, *Tao Te Ching,* "The master does her work thoroughly and lets go, letting whatever happens, happen." When nothing is forced, little remains undone.

In considering the balance between giving and receiving, helping others and developing alongside them, realize there is a difference between negligence and disinterest, or laziness—ignoring, avoiding, and denying—on one hand, and respectful distance and noninterference/nonaggression on the other. The key, perhaps, is being both caring and interested enough to strive consistently to discern what is actually going on, wanted, and needed. Through objective and disinterested yet keen truth-seeking and truth-telling, we can proactively engage in healing and restoring the world using active compassion and effective skillful means, rather than simply reactive or compulsive manipulation based on our own limited understanding, biased partiality, or selfish desires.

As for myself, I don't belong to any organized religion, I'm a Buddhist! I like to remember the Buddha's wise advice not to teach unless asked, to go only where invited, to contribute rather than convert others, to limit one's own needs, and to treat people with respect, tolerance, and lovingkindness. Remembering this guidance will go a long way to help us sustain our balance while helping others. Intervention is a large concept and needs considerable thought, clarity, and purity of heart to effectively carry it out.

Over two thousand years ago in China, Confucius taught us how to be a Superior Person, an impeccable individual, a real mensch, through ethical discipline and wise living—for the purpose of finding happiness and meaning, serenity, contentment, and genuine well being. He said:

> To put the world right in order, we must first put the nation in order; to put the nation in order, we must first put the family in order; to put the family in order, we must first cultivate our personal life, we must first set our hearts right.

Epilogue

THOUGHT EXPERIMENT: A QUESTIONING MEDITATION

Now let's practice the art of questioning with a simple and practical thought experiment in the form of a meditation practice. This is how we can learn to reflect, introspect, ponder, inquire, seek the good and true, and contemplate more deeply. My Concord neighbor Ralph Waldo Emerson said, "What lies behind us and what lies before us are tiny matters compared to what lies within us."

Sit comfortably; perhaps close your eyes. Take a deep breath or two and relax . . . Slow down, breathe slowly, and relax a little more . . . Release the tension, and relax.

Breathe, smile, focus, let go and let be, and relax. . . .

Stop doing, and settle back into just *being*. Leave some room for things to settle and clarify themselves, without effort, without your direction or intercession. Let go and let Buddha do it. Simply let it all happen. No need to make things fall into place. Let them go; perhaps wherever they fall can be the right place, for now.

Trust the innately healthy and whole, spiritual part of yourself. Open to the wisdom of openness, acceptance, and *allowing*.

Just breathe, focus, turn inwards, observe. Befriend yourself—smile and relax. Settle closer to your radiant inner self, deeper than personality and self-concept.

Don't get lost. Stay right there. Be transparent to yourself. Take care, be aware.

Breathe, let go—let come and go . . . Let be. Just be for a few moments, minutes, an eternity even . . . Enjoy the peace and serenity, the joy and harmony of natural meditation.

Once you've arrived and settled down a bit, turn the spotlight, the searchlight, *inward*. Think about something you would really like, above all else, to better understand, to comprehend, to penetrate in terms of the deeper mysteries of life—beyond who is going to win the next election or playoffs, or what the winning lottery number will be. Guess, speculate, or intuit: What is the nagging question that perplexes you when you are alone at night or have a break in your busy schedule and time to turn inward and look deeper into the meanings, purposes, paradoxes, mysteries, and deepest issues of life in general and of your life in particular? Ask yourself: What is the biggest question, my greatest existential question, the one thing I really want and need to understand?

If you climbed the highest mountain or went to the holiest holy lands to meet the wisest person in the world—the Buddha, Jesus, Socrates, Lao Tzu—what one question would you ask? (In Texas, they ask: What would Willy do?) What other question might you ask? Make it up! Free associate, don't edit—no one is watching or listening, judging or grading your response here.

Leave some room, beyond obsessive thought and analysis, and see what comes up from deeply within; observe what's on your mind. Uninhibitedly open the Pandora's Box of your audacious, outrageous, questioning heart. Your genuine questions will come.

Ask the question, and stay with it. Live into it. Let it ask you, too.

Breathe it in and breathe it out. Keep breathing, exploring and inquiring. Unknowing is an integral part of the practice.

Contemplate, ponder, meditate. Ask.

Stay with it. Just *stay.*

Your answers will come.